With kind
good wishes
from
Margery
Christmas, 1990

"the dusty beads from the post-office window" - 1922

(see page 12)

Victorian Mother

Edwardian Daughter

by
Margery Lea

BREWIN BOOKS

First published May 1990
by K.A.F. Brewin . Books, Studley, Warwickshire.

ISBN 0 947731 67 9

The front cover portaits are as follows:
Upper portrait - the author's mother, aged 21
Lower portrait - the author, aged 21

Typeset in Baskerville 11pt.
and made and printed in Great Britain by
Supaprint (Redditch)Ltd., Redditch, Worcs.

CONTENTS

BY THE SAME AUTHOR:

"These Days" — Wilding 1966

"Some Holy-Days and Home" — Outpost Publications 1975

"Pictures in our eyes" — Feather Publications 1983

"Diet and Health" — Awaiting Publication

INTRODUCTION

I was a child of five reigns, with memories of past events, states of mind, and visions that seem ever present as I write today. Why is nostalgia always sad? Memories of happy times are sad memories; is it because they are past and never likely to return?

We were children of what would be called today a 'caring' home - - - over-caring perhaps, as reflections on my mother and her maternal methods will show. An ordinary family we were, middle-class, I suppose, with a modest income that demanded careful living, sacrifices, and saving. We produced professional men and women who did well in several fields . . army, church, medicine, education. There were a few canons, and dons, a Director of Music, a Harley Street specialist, an Inspector of Schools, some lawyers, teachers, and assorted clergymen, and authors. One cousin was the Chief Engineer on board "Tiger" during the fateful meeting of Ian Smith and Harold Wilson. Another was chief Medical Officer to the S.E. Asian Forces under the command of Lord Mountbatten. A third had the honour of anaesthetising the Royal children when they had their tonsils out. Apart from a few learned books, some wartime Mentions in Dispatches, and a sprinkling of Palace Awards, I don't think any of them was particularly notable or in the public eye.

My father was a civil engineer, and we were the 'poor relations', a fact which my mother was deeply. . . but shyly, not bitterly. . . conscious of, and of which she never ceased to remind us. My brother was a scientist, and up to his retirement was the metallurgist in charge of the research laboratories at a large shipping firm in Birkenhead. At school he lapped up chemistry and physics with joyful ease, and without seeming to do any work at all. But the arts and languages rather bored him, as they enslaved me. In our later schooldays, he coached me in chemistry and I him in Shakespeare, Tennyson and Charles Lamb and other set books.

My own career was rather haphazard, and there will be more of that later. My father's work necessitated a good deal of travel, and in our childhood days we lived in a great many different houses all over the country, and attended as many different schools.   This, today, would be considered unsettling, but in spite of the fact that they all had different methods and different standards, I think it did us more good than harm.

Why then write about such an ordinary home and ordinary family?   I think they can only be of interest to the marvelling young and the reminiscent old, since our country and our world have undergone such huge changes since the 1914 war.

The forced emancipation of women;   the raising to a new life-style of what were then called the 'lower orders'. . . though I blush to write such words. . . the 'caring' state replacing the 'caring' family;   ominous hints of progressive ideas in education;   the overturn of simple faith by unbalanced scientific invention . . . all these were factors in the revolution in attitudes to life, and modes of living.

"How we lived then" . . . near history it might be called; and a sort of sad longing for all the good things that are past, the hardships, the contentments, the sturdy acceptance of life's 'unfairness', inspires the writer of these simple domestic chronicles.

My mother, a Victorian girl and woman in every sense, was born into a boisterous family of brothers and one bright sister with a modern outlook.   Her own mother was truly Victorian in date, and yet with a free spirit, an enquiring mind, and a zest for all that was amusing, interesting and improving.   In such a home was my mother brought up, attending a genteel private school for young ladies, and left it to remain at home, until snatched from her mother's care at the age of twenty, shy, inexperienced, into the arms of a young engineer whom she met at a church social.   And so she got married, and after three years produced two children, no doubt with great surprise, and of whom I am one.

My mother in her wedding-dress, 1902

CHAPTER I

OUR VERY EARLY YEARS

In 1964, at the time of another of our many removals, it was the style to have bare cream-washed walls in every room. Pictures of any kind were simply unfashionable; and among many household goods cast out were a number of delightful watercolours in delicate gold frames, some executed by a friend of the family. Among these. . . and the discarding of it is much regretted. . . was a lovely portrait of my mother in her wedding-dress. I don't think the painting itself was very expert, and was probably taken from a photograph, which I still have. The photo was taken on her wedding, and in both portraits she looked elegantly beautiful in an off-the-shoulder gown composed of many frills of silk crepe-de-chine and Brussels lace, with a pink rose in her bosom. Her hair was indeed a crowning glory, a golden chestnut with a natural wave and delicate fringe on her forehead, the whole so crisp and lively as to form a sort of golden auriole. Her eyes were large and liquid, and oh, so sad, so very sad, as though she bore the sufferings of the world. . . and this, a wedding portrait!

She was submissive and obedient to our Father; gentle, kindly and polite to friends. My mother was an accomplished pianist, a skilful needlewoman, and a successful gardener. How strange, then, that her 'duty' to us weighed so heavily upon her as to make her discipline so terribly severe. No one who did not live with her could possibly guess at the anxious fears that beset her, or understand the atmosphere of foreboding and apprehension that she managed to create in our home. She was fearful of so many things that it often seems to me, looking back over a long life, that she was fearful of life itself.

These apprehensions totally dominated our young lives. Her phobias were trivial and mostly domestic, but so insistently and sternly were her edicts drilled into our immature minds that it never occurred to us to question or ridicule them. And of course we were too young to appreciate that all was done in total dedication to our welfare. The psychological aspect of rearing children was wholly beyond her horizons, and I, in particular, developed from toddler to adolescent with the conviction that life would prove to be mostly miserable, difficult and dangerous.

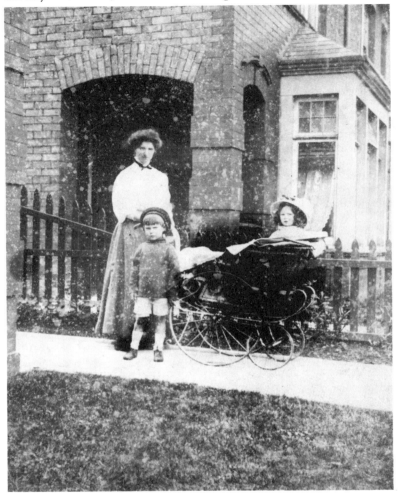

In Newcastle-on-Tyne, 1906-07

All the homely examples of life's perils come readily to mind: thunderstorms were occasions for the greatest alarm; to hold a steel knife or any metal object near an uncurtained window was to court instant death. Dogs were all dangerous . . . barking ones were to be skirted or run away from, friendly ones never touched. Vague hints of terrible diseases

2

resulting from their bites fortified these stringent rules. Cows or horses at pasture were also to be avoided. One did not walk through any field where even the mildest-looking herd was grazing. To walk alone outside the garden gate after dusk was asking for a sinister and unmentionable fate, for "nasty men would jump out of hedges". How often I heard that pronouncement, fraught with menace, yet how little was such a warning needed in those days!

Illness resulting from *chill* was another threat to my freedom and comfort. My poor mother had a real phobia about wearing warm and sufficient clothing. "Wool next the skin" were words written on my heart as was "Calais" on that of Mary Tudor. Our school uniform was brown and included long ribbed woollen stockings of merciless toughness; but these could be replaced by white socks in summer at the parents' discretion. Only in the most tropical heatwave was I allowed to obtain this blessed relief. How miserable I felt in my thick scrubby hose when all the other girls were sporting their cool white socks! The more so as the rapidly-felting legs became so firm as almost to inhibit knee-bending; and being supported by short suspenders to a Liberty bodice, the latter was drawn taut as armour over what should have been a budding figure. So convinced was my mother of the rashness of this vital exposure of the legs that importuning with heartfelt tears only brought me a caning on the back of the legs, administered by my father at mother's direction. "And I hope *that* will teach you not to keep worrying us about it!" All strictures regarding health were fortified with the words, "And if you disobey me and get ill as a result, *I* shall not nurse you!" Knowingly to have contacted someone with a "nasty catching disease" left me with a heavy burden of fear and guilt.

Even comestibles at the table did not escape the horrors associated with cows, bulls, lightning, chill winds, strange dogs, insufficient clothing, childish infections, and 'nasty men jumping out of hedges'. Stringy vegetables, for instance, rhubarb, celery, and suchlike, must be cut into very small pieces and eaten with caution, for the strings were dangerous and if they went wrong inside, could wrap themselves round your heart and you would die.

"Oh, no mother, they couldn't!" we would dare to say. "Oh, yes, they say so!" 'They' were the impeccable authority on whom mother based all her pronouncements. Stone fruits were also of the stuff of drama. Whenever we had damsons, my mother would rise from the table with a crimson face, announce dramatically that she 'had swallowed a stone', and retire hurriedly muttering the word 'appendicitis'. I don't know what she did in her absence, but I soon stopped picturing the grisly operation, as my father continued calmly eating his meal, and mother soon returned and resumed eating hers. She must have swallowed hundreds of stones, but I never knew her suffer any bad effects.

And talking of food, to leave any on one's plate was strictly forbidden. To fail to consume any sort or quantity that mother thought desirable was to court illness from undernourishment. "You will eat up that rice-pudding if you sit there till three o'clock!" Why three was always zero hour for sanctions I don't know, but many a time I sat there and those words too are graven on my heart.

My mother's preoccupation with positive health was intensified when coping with the problems of feeding the family in the first World War. Up to then we were amply stuffed with porridge, lentil soup, rabbit stew (rabbits being then fourpence each) nauseous boiled milk, Scott's Emulsion, and, as a precaution against costiveness, a delightful concoction called "Castols", cod-liver-oil somehow deodourised and compacted into little chocolate-flavoured squares. I still have one of the elaborate tin boxes in which they were packed, and use it for keeping spare buttons.

But the new and exceptional experience of the war threw light on a totally different side of my mother's character. In the 1914 war my father was in France, and she had to cope alone with what must have been very difficult circumstances, shortage of money being, I am sure, not the least of them; and shortage of food a daily problem. Rationing was not introduced till late in the war, and even the most basic foods were hard to come by. Meat we had only once or twice a week, eggs were scarce, fish and butter non-existent. We all shared the standing in queues for ½lb. of rice or a ¼ of margarine . . . and nasty it then was . . . or a few potatoes. Dried peas and lentils and dried apple-rings figured largely in our diet, but these too were scarce. Fuel was in short supply, and we were mostly cold. An old photo shows us all looking like inmates of Belsen. Yet I have no recollection of my mother ever uttering a murmur of complaint, fear, or anxiety. She simply kept steadfastly on doing her best for all of us under great hardships.

Later on in life I thought I detected in her a small capacity to laugh at herself. When my father offered her a glass of wine or sherry it was, "Oh, no, no, no, I couldn't possibly! It goes to my head. We. .lll, just a little, a very, very little!" Then she sat, pink and complacent, consuming a full glass, and hinting, with a slight smile, "that a little more, might be . . . . . ."

At one stage during our very early schooldays, there started the nervous ritual known as 'going out of church'. Halfway through the service my mother, looking shy and distressed, rose from her pew with much rustling of skirts, whispered to my father, "I feel faint!" and they both passed down the aisle and out of the church. Soon afterwards my father returned; we saw the service through and duly went home to find my mother attending to the dinner in perfect health. This, to us, embarrassing performance, was neither explained nor commented upon. We never dared ask, and never knew what happened to mother during her absence from church.

Linked with this memory is that of another Sunday ritual, enjoyable, but with painful associations for me. Straight from church father took us on a 'nature walk'; armed with magnifying glass and a nature book called "Eyes and no Eyes", he led us through field, lane, and woodland, pointing out and explaining every leaf, flower, seed, stone and bird, and gathering specimens to preserve at home in their various ways. This walk was pursued, of course, in our Sunday clothes, which meant an Eton suit for my brother, and for me, painful 'best' shoes. I can picture those shoes now . . . a golden fawn with an instep strap fastened with two pretty pearl buttons. But the toes were narrow and pinched horribly; I limped home each Sunday complaining of the pain. My mother's inconsistency, considering her pathological anxiety for our health, should have surprised me; but of course we never dared question any parental edict. "They are the right size", my mother repeated each Sunday, "I can't think why you don't like them, they're so pretty; it's only the newness." And so I went on suffering, and associating the beauties of nature with painful feet.

Later on, in adolescence, chilblains, ear-ache, catarrh and fallen arches added to my misery; but never was I taken to a doctor, or treated to anything but minor palliatives and a sadly shaken head. Looking back, I realise that my mother must have had a real fear of doctors; she herself never visited or received a visit from one, and much later in life I realised that she not only had an inborn but well-masked capacity for endurance, but that the stroke that finally ended her life might have been prevented by earlier treatment. Ill-health in any form was like a fearsome bogeyman to her, and she chose to shut her eyes tight against it whoever might be the unfortunate victim.

Several of us VIth Formers had a 'crush' on the School Captain, who was also Captain of Games. Edith her name was, a red-faced, wholesome looking girl as ever I remember, with keen blue eyes and hefty calves. Our geography mistress, a jolly, sparkling blond beloved by everyone, was also friendly with Edith. When the latter had unaccountably to be in a private nursing-home, Miss G. invited three of us to go along with her to visit the invalid. I dare not mention the word 'nursing-home' to my mother, and hoped that some flash of inspiration on my part would explain my late return home after school. But, alas, the most severe probing and questioning on her part had to elicit the truth. I had actually been to visit someone sick in hospital without her knowledge! The horror in her eyes! "You didn't go *near* her? Did you sit on her bed?" (Yes, I had.) "You didn't. . . . *kiss* her?" In vain I explained that Edith had had a small operation on a tendon in her knee.

Another incident came to mind, earlier than my adolescent difficulties. A new family came to live in our road, and I became friends with the daughter who went to my little dame school . . . a pale child, not very healthy-looking, but never ill or absent so far as I knew. We became 'sworn' best friends, as small girls are apt to do. One day, most unusually, my parents went for a short Saturday walk, leaving us playing alone in our front garden. They returned to find us outside the gate, looking for them, our arms lovingly twined round each other's waists. I remember my mother's sharp dismissal of Eva, 'home to tea, *at once*', and I was quickly escorted up the path, hearing the words, "most unwholesome. . . unhealthy. . ." Totally unaware of having done anything wrong or disobedient, I was once again filled with a sense of guilt and fear of something unknown.

And yet I remember with pleasure our regular Sunday evening entertainment, listening to my mother playing Chopin, Schumann, and Beethoven, my father adding a violin obbligato, or singing to her accompaniment, the sentimental ballads of the time.

My poor, dear, dutiful mother, who made life so hard for herself, she never did anything for enjoyment or for fun. . . if we went for a walk, it was to take 'deep breaths for our health'. Our 'stocking presents' at Christmas consisted of a toothbrush, a piece of soap, or a new face-flannel! "Wool next the skin" and "A girl is best at home with her mother" seemed to be the chief two formulae on which she based her system of child-care. She was life-denying, not life enhancing. I had the impression in childhood, that if anything was pleasurable, amusing or interesting, it was best *not* to do it than to do it. Hence the narrowing of our lives to school, sleep, clothes, health, scant toys, a few worthy hobbies; but plenty of books and outdoor exercise. . . my father saw to that. . and very occasionally a short holiday in some quiet rooms at the nearest seaside place.

On one of our modest holidays at Lytham-St. Annes, I remember seeing on the green 'stray' above the beach small groups of men marching and drilling. They wore dark suits and bowler hats, and presented arms with furled umbrellas. This was the start of the 1914 war, when there were no uniforms, arms, or weapons for the hastily conscripted army, and, it was said, only three rickety planes.

Women poured into the munition factories . . . the first time that women, apart from domestic workers, school-teachers, and 'lady typewriters', had gone out on gainful employment in any numbers; and no doubt the start of female liberation.

But now the war was over, the Armistice signed by the Germans, and ratified by the Treaty of Versaille in 1919. The munitions ladies went home; the war heroes returned to find no jobs, and went about selling carpet-sweepers, and encyclopaedias from door to door.

My father returned from France; there was more food about; and we moved to a larger house in a leafy road nearer to my school.

CHAPTER II

MY SCHOOL IN MANCHESTER –
ADOLESCENT FRIENDSHIPS

My school! There I was totally happy; its strict rules and disciplines neither irked nor aroused resentment in me as did, sometimes, those of home. I loved every moment of every lesson; chemistry perhaps less so, as we had an extremely severe science mistress, who set us staggering amounts of homework, which took time from what I considered more desirable pursuits such as Eng. Lang. and Lit., French and Latin, which I adored.

I enjoyed tussling with algebra, Euclid, trigonometry, logarithms, calculus. I loved history, geography, botany, grammar, music, art, scripture, nature study, folk-dancing. We played games too, hockey, basket-ball, tennis, cricket. How all these subjects were crammed into our day, I cannot imagine. A copy of the complicated but rigid timetable was pinned inside the lid of each desk, and we moved, in decorous crocodiles, from our 'home' classroom to other rooms for each different lesson. After assembly and prayers classes walked back in orderly file to their own rooms, headed by the class monitor, who stood at the door inspecting each girl to see that she was tidy and correctly dressed. There followed ten minutes of brain-teasing mental arithmetic and of spelling, this taking place in every class except upper and lower sixth.

The senior Latin mistress happened to be our form mistress, a large, busty handsome woman like a Roman matron, and terrifying. In our class the ritual was as follows: The mistress seized the long iron poker from the small fireplace in the corner of the room, and pointing it at each girl in turn she shot round the class like a Gatling gun, firing off numbers . . . . "9x5. .plus 7. . plus 16. . . plus 6. . plus 21 . . plus 11 . . . plus 15. . 51. ." and so on.

This bracing session over, we sitting on the edge of our seats with glazed eyes and thumping hearts, there followed SPELLING. Each girl had in her desk a tall think book containing a single column of 'difficult' words on each page. Two minutes were given to study a selected page, and then spelling out began. The poker was brought into action again, but this time the girls were picked on at random, something like this: *"You,* spell 'hieroglyphics', *you,* 'ventriloquist', *you,* 'effervescence', *you,* 'vicissitude', *you,* 'iridescent', *you,* 'allotment', the stumblers being sent to the bottom of the class. The mistress was quite good-natured under her seeming ferocity, and we quite enjoyed it as a game; and with brains jerked into top gear, we were ready to start formal classroom lessons.

We had a splendid gymnasium, but our gym mistress was regrettably old. She had a mass of grizzled hair stuffed into a net, and pince-nez balanced aslant a sharp nose. Before each lesson she retired behind a screen and emerged wearing the briefest of circular skirts which she called, quite seriously, her 'decency'. Needless to say she could not vault over a horse or shin up the ropes and do a Flying Angel down them. A daring girl had to be chosen to demonstrate new routines at her direction.

Sports Day at school in Hull - author eclipsed by Sunday-best hat and long white gloves.

9

We did a lot of play-acting, which I greatly relished. Once, in Form III Alpha, we performed a fairy play which I myself had written, and in which I was cast as the Rose Fairy. I remember in that role trying to keep out of sight behind a cardboard tree, wearing, as I was, an old white cotton dress stuck all over with blobs of bright pink paper. Later I rejoiced in proper hired costumes for "She stoops to Conquer", "School for Scandal", and other worthy and educational plays, not forgetting Shakespeare.

Then we had wonderful ceremonial days, Parents' Day, Sports Day, Speech Day, Empire Day, May Day, and "End-of-Term, when we bellowed out songs from the "Scottish Students' Song book", and tearfully wound up with "Forty Years On", which, strange to say, was our school song. We were proud of our school, faithful to its traditions, and tried to uphold its honour at all times and places.

We had a wonderful headmistress. She had a pile of orange hair, white at the temples, a hooked nose like a parrot, small cold grey eyes, and a hint of a ginger moustache. When she had made a pronouncement, she threw back her head and closed her eyes with an air of finality that settled the matter for all time. Any unfortunate summoned to her study could be seen trembling outside her door, no doubt kept waiting to break her nerve.

One habit of mind and behaviour inculcated in me by both home and school dies very hard with me; that of respecting, to the point of awe, even of abasement, Authority in any form. Our schoolteachers, clergy, doctors, elderly relatives, these, as a matter of course. But any official, however lowly his particular field, had to command our respect, even fear. Thus, anyone in a peaked cap, be it tram-conductor, milkman, postman, station-porter, or park-keeper, was someone to whom we owed polite obedience and respect on all occasions.

It can be imagined, then, how once in the Lower VIth, when I was commanded to present myself to the Head, my knees shook with fear. What crime had I committed? I could think of none, but my apprehensions increased to panic proportions when I saw, present also in the holy of holies, the Latin mistress whom I had earlier shocked by an episode connected with a school theatre outing. . . . but this is another story.

"When we requested your parents to come for an interview with us yesterday afternoon . . . " began the Head, and I stared at her with glazed eyes. . . "we hoped very much that they would cooperate with us in preparing you for Oxford. We assured them repeatedly that you would have

10

no difficulty in gaining an Open Scholarship to read Modern Languages. . . ." At this point I saw her face sag into bewilderment as she saw she had made a tactless error. "Did you know about this?" she asked. "No", I said weakly as if in a dream. "Then they seem to have other plans for your future", she finished coldly; and the matter was never mentioned again.

Of course my parents had never told me of this interview. The Head's disclosing of it I suppose had been in the hopes of my adding my persuasion to theirs, but little did they know my parents. I decided the time had come to speak out, and with much trepidation I told them of my surprising encounter with the Head, adding a weak, "So -- er -- what about it? Could I go? Can I enter?" My father was very angry at their having told me of their meeting at the school, and my mother annoyed at their inciting me to rebellion and to the promotion of ridiculous and unattainable ambitions.

"Your brother will be going to University, and that is all we can afford!"

"A girl does not need a career."

"A daughter is best at home with her mother!"

How sad was my very last End-of-Term! Saying good-bye to the mistresses, to my friends, many of whom were going to University, and to my beloved school! Going forth into the wide world, with aspirations crushed, and with no definite plans for a career!

But to return to my mother's code of behaviour in other than scholastic spheres. It is not difficult to imagine her attitude to our emotional development during adolescence. "Emotion" is a word perhaps best left out altogether, for she seemed to have a horror of being involved in any situation that gave rise to it, be it love, joy, fear, or any other manifestation of human feeling. "Do you think she . . . er . . *likes* him?" my mother would murmur about some blissfully engaged young woman. Thank heaven there was no T.V. or radio in those days, as it would have been torture indeed to have sat en famille to receive the like of today's projections. She would hurry from the room on pretext of some urgent domestic task, if the mildest emotion or awkward question threatened to raise its ugly head. I remember her doing so when, on one occasion only, I having received a certain amount of no doubt inaccurate information, absolutely *dared* her to answer my question, "Where *do* babies come from, Mother?"

My great friend at school was one of a large family of girls whose father was a professor at the University. They lived in a tall town house nearby, and used to give jolly dances in their large first-floor drawing-room. As my brother was friendly with an older sister and played tennis with her, I was allowed to attend these functions. Their mother was very care-free, liberal-minded and witty; and the girls were all artistic.

They used to do up the drawing-room as a sort of cave, with fish-net and witch-balls draped about; with lighted candles in skulls and pumpkin-faces, and joss-sticks burning incense in corners. The girls used to float about in silk Batik scarves which they themselves tie-dyed in the bath, and sold to Liberty's.

My brother used to admire another school-friend of mine called Jean, and I used to invite her to the house so that he could meet her. This led to an older brother of hers, a handsome student of architecture at the University, becoming friendly with me; and the four of us sometimes went to the pictures together when there was a suitable film such as Scott's Expedition to the Antarctic, when we paid ninepence each to sit in the best seats.

There came an occasion when my parents decided to go away for a few days, actually to visit a sick relative, leaving us alone in the house. Enjoying this unwonted freedom, we decided one evening to abandon studying and go to visit our friends. Their mother seemed quite happy to leave us alone, which my mother would *never* have done; and shut the door firmly on the room where we innocently played ping-pong, sang songs round the piano, and consumed weak tea and scones which Jean brought in from the kitchen. Daringly we stayed very late, and Willy presented me, on our departure, with a rose from a vase on the piano. Subsequently he once walked me to the Free Lending Library, and bought me a dusty string of beads which had hung for months in the window of the local Post Office. Apart from that, I don't remember ever being in his company except with the other two.

Then, one day, we found ourselves in dire trouble. Their mother, never having met our mother before, unexpectedly called on her one Sunday afternoon. I was summoned to the drawing-room, where our visitor without preamble, demanded to know if I and her son Willy intended to get engaged to be married. Because if so "it was not with her approval, we were too young and ought to wait." Astounded and dismayed at her extraordinary question, I could only stare speechlessly at both of them. I simply could not find words to tell them that in my wildest dreams I, or we, had never thought or talked of such a thing; that he had never so much as put an arm round my waist, that it was the mildest of companionships. . . .

My mother, red-faced and tearful with shock, obviously thought something terrible had happened in her absence, as she kept wringing her hands and saying, "We should never, never have left them alone!"

The friendship was banned forthwith, their house put out of bounds, my brother forbidden to see Jean, and I to speak to her at school. I don't remember that we minded very much, our chief feeling being of resentment against such a silly and tactless woman who could make so much trouble for us, and what prompted her to act thus we never discovered. But later, Willy went to Paris to study art, and started to write me long letters full of descriptions of cathedrals, and these never received any reply because they were confiscated and burnt, and so the matter finally ended.

About this time I won, with minimum effort and rather less enthusiasm, a scholarship to a Training College of Domestic Science and Arts. My father grudgingly conceded that it sounded quite a suitable training for a girl and that I might as well make use of it. I did not care for the work. . . there was too much chemistry and very boring practical work. . . but we were affiliated to the Students' Union of the University and enjoyed quite a lot of fun with them as well as with our own societies.

At the end of the three years' course I was determined to leave home and bewildered my parents by refusing a post in my home town. I made forty applications to places all over the British Isles, writing out by hand three testimonials to each, together with lists of qualifications, now known as a curriculum vitae. This prodigious effort resulted in four unsuccessful interviews, and finally a post in a small country town in Buckinghamshire. Enquiries in a corner shop led to my getting two nice private rooms with a motherly land-lady who cooked for me the food I sparingly bought. A College Maintenance Grant had enabled me to buy nice new clothes for the first time; but now, a salary of two pounds, seventeen shillings, and sixpence a week, covered all my expenses quite comfortably, with a margin to buy a weekly National Savings Certificate.

CHAPTER III

STAYING AT GRANDMOTHER'S IN SHEFFIELD

Very often the modern grandmother, tailored, blue-rinsed, and well-preserved, seems to belong to no particular generation. She whips round her uncluttered bungalow or flat, and goes off to her golf or her committees. In dress, occupation and outlook, she is merely a slightly maturer edition of her daughter, and often looks little older. Indeed, when Granny is smart in well-cut tweeds, with shoulder-bag and other chic accessories, and grand-daughter is in pavement-length Laura Ashley print, with a fringed shawl and hair in a bun, there is a great confusion of generations, and granny is left bereft of all the endearing and estimable qualities of grannydom.

How different was the grandmama of my young days! An enchanting aura of the past surrounded her; her attics and cellars harboured exciting relics of other days. My paternal grandmother was about eighty four years old in 1910 when I was five, so she must have been born in about 1826. My mother's mother was much younger and not at all strict; and it was to her home that we most enjoyed going.

Her house stood on a steep slope and had an extra storey at the back. How intrigued we were to pass from deep, dark cellars straight onto a sunny garden; thence to gain the kitchen by an external wooden stair like a ship's ladder. That kitchen was our favourite haunt. It had a huge open Yorkshire range which was blackleaded every day. There were brass knobs and trimmings, and a high steel fender which was burnished with emery-paper. In the recess by the range was a shallow brown slopstone. One tap, when coaxed, loosed a feeble trickle of water straight down an open waste-pipe. A second, more beautiful brass tap was connected by snake-like plumbing to the fire-boiler.

After every washing-up, in a tin basin, the sink was scoured with rotten-stone; and the taps polished with a muddy liquid from a black stout-bottle. This was a concoction of pumice powder, whiting and fine ashes, mixed with paraffin and a dash of ammonia. A whiff from Jennie's 'strong bottle' brought choking tears to our eyes.

On one end of the massive sycamore wood dresser was clamped a rotary knife-cleaning machine . . . . the latest type, that eliminated entirely the use of messy bathbrick boards. We children never tired of turning its handle, and were held largely responsible for the wafer-like condition of Grannie's knife-blades.

Then there was a huge deal table covered with a fringed chenille cloth; a rag rug by the fire; a plush-seated rocking-chair; and a large black tomcat called Sooty, but for whom mice and beatles would have abounded.

With it all was associated a permanent and endearing smell, a smell compounded of oilcloth and scrubbed wood; of good home-made bread; and baskets of freshly-starched cotton underwear, crimped pillow-cases and table-linen like white marble.

It was Jenny who, one evening, accidently shut Sooty into the oven along with the large earthenware dish of porridge which was set to 'cree' gently every night. We heard her scream with horror as she opened the oven at breakfast-time, and Sooty fell at her feet steaming all over. He loped into the vegetable garden, licking his fur, and shaking his whiskers in the early sunshine. Sooty quickly recovered, but ever afterwards I had a queer feeling about Granny's oven.

Jenny was Granny's housemaid, and one of the permanent fixtures of her kitchen. She came from Worksop . . . or was it Workington? Both places were firmly linked in my mind with slopping pails and blackened housemaid's boxes. She wore a morning print, surmounted by starched white cap and apron. In the afternoon she changed into her black 'stuff', with an embroidered apron and frill, in which she answered the clanging bell, and 'waited on' during Granny's "At Homes".

No one questioned the suitability, on hygienic grounds, of Granny's time- and fire-worn cooking vessels. They were all stained and 'crazy' and even when cleanly washed, exuded a pungent aroma. No modern dish ever had such a smell, but it was to me the quintessence of all the hot and satisfying puddings that ever were made.

One particular basin, whose multiple cracks were etched in rich black, was always used for the 'pobbies' (hot bread-and-milk) with which sufferers from colds or stomach-ache were sent early to bed. Perhaps Granny plied us too lovingly with home-made treacle toffee, and good Yorkshire tharfe-cake; and toothache was irrevocably associated with Fuller's iced walnut cake which appeared on the table at every birth-day.

15

Our keenest disappointment regarding food occurred on each of our regular duty visits, one each holiday, to some distant cousins, 'Mrs. Hunt-and-Edith'. For this occasion we had to leave our play, wash and dress tidily, which meant uncomfortably, join a rustling Granny and flower-hatted mother in the hall to wait for the horse-drawn carriage to appear, to take us on our journey. This was to the large house near the Botanical Gardens. This meant at least one very steep hill, and was quite exciting except when it was freezing and snowy, when the horse would stagger to the kerb and come to a stop, and I was quite certain that we would all roll backwards down the hill. I felt safer on my own legs, and we thoroughly enjoyed the few occasions that Mother and Granny dreaded, when the driver asked us all to dismount while he went to the horse's head and led it up the steepest part, drawing an empty carriage.

We were not allowed to play in the big garden even on a summer visit, but had to talk politely indoors. Mrs. Hunt was small and thin and old and didn't seem to matter much, but we didn't like Miss Edith who was pale with scraped-back hair and piggy eyes and shiny pince-nez. Tea was served in the dining-room on our visits on a huge, shining-white table with very few plates of food. But there was always a big, rich, iced and decorated cake.

Our eyes fastened on this, and we waited with sinking hearts for the little ritual that always preceded the pouring of the tea from the great silver pot. Mrs. Hunt reached for the cake and passed it to Miss Edith who, in turn, moved it to the farthest corner of the table, saying, "Yes, we won't cut the cake today, it is really much too rich for children."

Writing of horse-drawn carriages reminds me of straw in the suburban roads: not only was it laid over horses' 'jobbies' before being swept up, but was strewn thickly from pavement to pavement opposite the house of anyone seriously ill. People were more commonly nursed at home those days, with night and day nurses; and the doctor usually arranged for the straw to be laid so that the clop-clop of horses' hooves and the grating rumble of iron wheels should not disturb the patient.

I remember its being laid once in our quiet road. "Is it real country hay?" we asked, "Can we take some for our rabbits?"

"Certainly not," said Mother, "It is straw, not hay; poor Miss Amiel opposite is *very* ill, and not one wisp must be touched."

Horseless vehicles were just coming in; and some well-to-do friends of my parents invited us to share a ride in their new automobile. The four of us sat perched up on leather seats behind the driver, who wore a Norfolk jacket, a cap with ear-flaps, and goggles over his eyes. My mother had a flowing scarf over her large hat, and mine was tied down with a tight ribbon.

I remember we drove through a pretty blue-bell wood on a high, narrow muddy track beside a stream. Mr. Chipperfield, for that was his name, seemed to jerk the steering-wheel round and round rather a lot, and also constantly turned his head to explain the wonders of his vehicle and to listen to our 'ooh's' and ah's of delight; but I was nervous that the carriage, with no obvious means of propulsion, might take a sudden jerk down the bank into the stream, especially as we were, as he told us, travelling at least ten miles an hour.

My father, although an engineer, never fancied one of these noisy, dust-and-fume-enveloped vehicles; and it was many, many years before a bull-nosed Morris became my precious possession.

Sometimes we went shopping with Granny. She bought pure creamy lard in bladders which we called 'bald heads'; peas at 1/9 the peck; twenty eggs for a shilling, and good pie-beef at 4d per pound.

As for Granny herself, she was a cosy person, with auburn kiss-curls and a cushiony bosom upholstered in pleated satin. She had a fine soprano voice, a talent for mimicry which kept us convulsed with laughter, and a passion for reading Byron at the breakfast-table. Also, she used face-powder. It was whitish in tone and smelt very 'French'. We knew what 'French' was because we had an aunt married to a Frenchman and living in Paris, and when they came on visits, mother said she was 'very French'. Granny's powder was kept in a shiny tartan box with a picture on the lid of Queen Victoria on her pony with John Brown at her side.

Granny was a widow in those days, but later she married again . . . a Swedish gentleman who was said to have spied for the Germans in the War, and who broke her heart. He wasn't shot by a firing-squad, which I think rather disappointed us, but we quickly picked up and made the most of the fact that he had gone to prison. The white face-powder and the Swedish spy together invested Granny with an aura of worldly sophistication which entranced my childish heart. What modern grandmother could compete with that?

Then Granny's garden afforded us endless pleasure. It was an odd exciting shape, with lots of mysterious little paths, and shrubs, and hiding-places; and it adjoined one belonging to another brother and sister called John and Sylvie. Their lawns and tall trees could be transformed at will into jungle or desert isle, or western prairie. On our side of the wall grew a mass of balsams, and our great delight was to touch off the miniature explosions from their dried seed-capsules.

There was no wireless in those days; 'motion pictures' were talked of, but we seldom went to see them. We made our own fun and games, and our memories are the longer and richer for it. Mine will always be associated with Granny's home . . . with the steaming tomcat, and the popping balsams, and the low stone wall over which we gazed into the Red Indian Territory of John and Sylvie's garden.

CHAPTER IV

A HALFPENNY BAR OF CHOCOLATE

When I was two-and-a-half . . . . and that was over 80 years ago . . I was given my first pocket money, a halfpenny a week.

Each Saturday morning, in the firm grasp of big brother, aged four, I was allowed to toddle to the village shop round the corner. We climbed some stone steps and opened the door to the sound of a loud clanging bell. The floor was of rough boards with hard shiny knots in them, and covered with sawdust.

Skipping-ropes and wooden hoops; and tops tied up with their whips, hung from the ceiling, along with sides of bacon, jugs, iron kettles and bedroom ware. I remember best the powerful smell, meaty and fruity, but with overtones of rabbit hutches and donkeys; and with strong whiffs of mother's medicine cupboard and grandmamma's basement kitchen.

On the counter bright pink celluloid dolls lay cheek-by-jowl with balls of brown wool, cards of bone buttons, and blocks of bathbrick for cleaning steel knives. Somewhere among the shoe-blacking and the monkey-brand soap was my goal - - - rows of brown cardboard boxes, their slightly battered lids turned back to display a tempting array of sweetmeats.

My halfpenny would have bought almost anything . . . two giant striped humbugs, several liquorice bootlaces, a chunk of black treacle toffee, or a generous fistful of coloured comfits.

But when my turn came, I repeated dutifully the formula I had been taught: "A-halfpenny-bar-of-milk-chocolate-without-nuts-please." The bar, unwrapped, of course, fragile, flat on one side, satisfyingly humped on the other, was selected from the open box, slipped into a tiny three-cornerd bag, and carefully taken home to be consumed after dinner.

Occasionally the chocolate was found to have a whitish bloom on it . . 'only with being in the window, my dear' . . . and sometimes it tasted, not surprisingly, of soap or paraffin;

but as complaints might have resulted in my losing it altogether, I soon learnt to put up with these assorted flavours.

Mass-produced ice-cream was unknown; so were ice-lollies; but in any case, little ladies did not, I was told, consume in the street sweetmeats that required to be *licked* or *sucked*; and nuts were (along with cheese and red meat) considered quite unsuited to infant digestions.

And so the trip to buy the halfpenny bar was the great event of my Saturdays, and the routine never varied.

* * * * *

School Days in Hull, 1914

At six years old my allowance had risen to threepence, of which one penny had to be saved in a black tin money-box with a tiny key.

Between eight and ten years old I had sixpence a week; but by now all sorts of moral principles were inextricably linked with the receipt of this princely sum. Twopence went into the black box; a penny towards church collection; and a penny to help 'poor little girls and boys in hospitals and orphanages'. As for large and important purchases, these became doubly desirable and precious, as they were paid for by painful savings, and the sacrifice of minor pleasures and possessions. If we wanted something badly enough, we had to go without something else to get it; and nothing was to be used or enjoyed until paid for.

Beloved books, toys and games purchased with such hardship acquired an almost mystic importance and permanence. "Uncle Tom's Cabin", "Grimm's Fairy Tales", and "Brer Rabbit" might get well thumbed, but carelessly or wantonly to damage the spine or loosen the cover was a major crime. Dolls had a lived-with appearance, but it was disaster if a skull got cracked, or sawdust trickled from a limb; or a pair of eyes fell with a sickening thud into the back of a pot head.

These rules about the care of our sacred possessions seemed to have but two exceptions. One was "Alice-in-Wonderland". An enlightened aunt sent us the newest edition, illustrated by Mabel Lucie Attwell; and her line drawings were allowed to fall victims to our brushes and crayons; for her chubby creatures were infinitely more tempting than Tenniel's dark black-and-white illustrations. My daughter, in her turn, admired the shocking pink pig-baby in the arms of the Duchess; and the brilliant crimson of the standard roses that were the result of our artistic efforts. While this helped to satisfy our continual demand for colouring-books, paint brushes presented no problem; these were made from my brother's hair, which was evidently of a suitable texture. My mother snipped off bits behind his ears, tied the little tuft with a firm wind of cotton round a matchstick, and deftly trimmed it to a point. We were perfectly satisfied with these substitutes for the Art shop's best sable, and the supply was inexhaustible.

The other exception to these stern rules about the care of property, I know not why, unless there was sex discrimination, was my brother's box of lead soldiers. He never fought battles with these in the accepted fashion, but put them on an old rusty shovel over our hot, red kitchen fire to melt. It was the same shovel that was used for popping corn and roasting chestnuts; but some instinct, or empirical study, must have assured him that the soldiers would melt long before the shovel did. His most notable experiment was at five years old, when he carried the churning puddle of grey metal to the cold tap 'to see what it would do'. After a fearful hiss and a tremendous clatter, he rushed in screaming, his face pitted, and his hair decorated with fragments of molten lead. The metal soldiers certainly played their part in his scientific education: he became a metallurgist in his mature years.

* * * * *

The habits of training of childhood die hard. My first proper dress allowance was laid out with exquisite care. My first meagre earnings were husbanded with such mathematical nicety to cover my bed-sitter and my food, that I nearly starved myself into an illness. Some modern children, to whom all is come-easy-go-easy, and who see their parents living on hire-purchase, could not begin to understand the reasons or necessities for these disciplines; but though we accepted and endured the rules, we enjoyed commensurate excitements and satisfactions.

No youngster in receipt of liberal cash, or sweetmeats and toys unlimited could appreciate the delights of spending - - and saving - - those niggardly but precious Saturday morning pennies.

CHAPTER V

YOUTHFUL READING

In a radio programme the other week the question was asked, "Do you remember actually learning to read?" Pondering on the answer, and at the same time seeing a review of a recently-published book called "Learning to Read" by Margaret Meek, prompted me to start reminiscing about our early introduction to the pleasures of books, when I was about eight years old.

We could certainly read simple words before going to our little dame school at about five or six years old; but my sharpest remembrance of that happy day was of my first official reading-book. It was thin, brown-cloth-covered, without illustrations, a dull little volume, but not only can I see its well-frayed pages as clearly as if I were handling it now, but experience again the sense of blissful satisfaction on reading its first sentences, "THE CAT SAT ON THE MAT". "THE DOG SAT ON THE RUG", in well-spaced black print. It proceeded to longer and more informative sentences, and was twinned with a sum book 2 + 2 = 4 which gave as much pleasure. There was also a book of poems called "On Linden Low", of which the title poem had an illustration of two little girls in Kate Greenaway dresses bowing to each other on a hilltop, with a round, raying sun behind them. This small sketch made me feel intensely the excitement of those early misty mornings that promise delicious hot summer days to come, an experience with me still.

There is a gap in my memory at this point, except for recollections of a lovely geography book replete with maps and lots of bright pink British Empire; also of a highly-prized botany exercise book whose lined pages alternated with pages of rough drawing-paper for leaf and flower paintings.

The study of the former was augmented by practical geography in the form of a large wooden tray with sand and clay to form isthmuses, islands, straits and promontaries. How exciting it was to gather round that board to watch our mistress form these features. Our knowledge was also fortified by 'nature walks', and again I recall the thrill of finding acorns, oak-galls, catkins, sticky horse-chestnut buds, rose-burrs, mistletoe, cowslips, and crysalids and butterflies, according to the season of the year.

My mind then goes to books at home, many preserved for our grand-children. . . "Peter Pan" of course, much-loved; the two "Alices", which I have never liked much, having always found it distasteful to see animals dressed as people and people as animals. Though, later, the charm of Beatrix Potter seemed to overcome this revulsion. The redeeming feature of our "Alice" was that it had line drawings which we filled in vigorously in bright waxy colours.

Later, I remember poring and doting over "Grimm's Fairy Tales", a grim-looking volume indeed, with dark brown cloth back, small print, and gloomy illustrations. As with my first reading-book, I carried it about with me everywhere, and couldn't bear to be parted from it except at bed and meal-times.

The Green, Red, Blue and Yellow Fairy Books, given as presents, were regarded as light reading; comics, mild, polite, and harmless as they then were, like 'sweets-between-meals', were strictly taboo. The "Waterbabies" was a great favourite, the stories of Mrs. Horatia Ewing, and, of course, "Little Lord Fauntleroy", a copy of which, dated 1886, I still have. It has strong dark red covers, imprinted with black and gold, and with beautiful pen illustrations. How I gloated and wept over the one entitled, "Shall I still be your boy even if I'm not going to be an earl?" asked Cedric.

Nature books we had in abundance, my favourite being "The Tale of Jack Rabbit" illustrated with photographs; and another called "Eyes and No Eyes" which my father required us to take with us on the 'nature walks' on which he led us. There was also "Physiography", all about the earth's crust, volcanoes, deltas, and tides; the phases of the moon, names and positions of the planets, Silurian rocks, artesian wells, sources of rivers, with lots of photos and drawings, another much-prized book, long since gone and out-of-print.

Later treasures I remember well were a dull-looking "Euclid". . . how satisfying those 'figs.' and Q.E.D.'s!. . . an English grammar, dark of cover and small of print; and a book called "Myths and Legends of Ancient Greece and Rome", which, besides having beautiful illustrations, summarised and clarified the 'divisions of labour', and seeming matrimonial tangles of the whole Pantheon. I wish I still had all three.

Moving towards adolescence, the books we loved and constantly re-read were all Kipling, Mark Twain, Ernest Bramah's "Wallet of Kai Lung", William Prescott's famous

"History of the Conquest of Peru", and Bulmer Lytton's "Last of the Barons". Anything by Scott, Barrie, Rider Haggard, Stevenson and S.R. Crockett went down very well.

Soon we were plunged into the required background reading for exams, and also devoured, somewhat indiscriminately, Hardy Thackeray, H.G. Wells, the Brontes, Jane Austen, Henry James, Galsworthy, Proust, Virginia Woolf and many others. I enjoyed Ivy Compton-Burnett, relishing her carefully-moulded, revealing and potent dialogue. Later I developed a passion for the curious romances of William Morris, such as "Well at the World's End", "The Story of the Glittering Plain" and others, the modern equivalent, I suppose, being the fantasies of T.H. White, C.S. Lewis, Mervyn Peake, and Ursula Le Guin. I also revelled in the novels of Mary Webb, now rather fashionable again, even if only in her native Shropshire, but now must confess to finding them less compelling. Of course we had to analyse Shakespeare's Plays to shreds, and commit to memory large slabs of Tennyson, Wordsworth, Arnold and Keats. We loved the travel books of H.M. Tomlinson, H.V. Morton, and the novels of Henry Williamson. Essayists were very popular then, and we enjoyed C.E. Montague, E.V. Lucas, and A.C. Benson. But, "Addison and Steele" and "Sir Roger de Coverley" were 'set' books, and I remember an occasion when our English mistress was genuinely amazed, in a good-natured manner, when we all suddenly burst forth in unison one day, declaring those gentlemen, together with Malvolio, Charles Lamb, and. . . especially. .*Falstaff.* . to be sickening, boring, horrible old men.

During a serious period of late teenage, I remember coping with Dunne's "Experiment with Time", William James' "Variety of Religious Experience", and, of course, Einstein's "Theory of Relativity", the admission of such tastes earning for me from a university pal of my brother's the comment, "What a formidable young woman your sister is!" not a promising remark from a handsome young man with a bright red sports car and a love of dancing!

One bookish incident of my early teens I remember with some surprise: we were revising for what would be the equivalent of O-levels, namely, Matriculation. My brother and I shared a playroom, in which we were allowed to do and keep anything we liked, except pets, which had to be in the outer wash-scullery. The playroom had plain, cream-washed walls, and I suddenly saw them as a marvellous, almost unlimited supply of exercise paper. How easy to memorise by writing everything on the walls with a soft lead pencil!

The end result was a wonderful mural. . . all four walls

completely covered as far as my arm would reach.   Huge
swathes of the major poets filled the centre, flanked by strips
of Latin translation.   Corners were neatly filled in with, here,
a poem of Rossetti, or there a scrap of trigonometry; a batch
of syntax next to "Dover Beach"; or some W.B. Yeats
nestling by geometry or calculus.

Algebraic equations were mixed up with Shakespeare's
sonnets.   Or a map of the Nile with dates of battles, and a
selection of chemical formulae.   I can see those walls in all
their detail, and often wonder what the next owners of the
house thought of this form of decor, as I don't remember
it being washed off before we left.

About that time I developed most inconveniently a
severe attack of mumps, and remember waking up one
morning with a painful and grotesquely swollen face.   Determined not to waste any time I set myself the task of learning
by heart a whole page of Tennyson's "Morte D'Arthur"
before my gruelly breakfast was brought up.   My poor
mother had to listen to a recital of it, word-perfect, I think
before I would start on the painfully unpalatable meal.

How fortunate we were to have a father who not only
took us on long and informative nature walks, but read to us
every Sunday afternoon from 'good books'.   He also
required us to gaze down his microscope when it was set up
with 'diatoms'. . specks which he said were in face-powder. . .
micro-sections of leaves and stems, or 'faults' in slivers of
metal.

I still think that being required to read the good solid
old masters in one's youth can only be a good thing; and I
remember being rather horrified when my daughter returned
home from school for the holidays furnished with a book list
for general reading prepared by their young English mistress,
and which contained not one 'classic'.   It was full of such
names as Stan Barstow, Nell Dunn, John Updike, Malcolm
Bradbury, John Braine, Kingsley Amis, and sundry rather
lightweight women novelists, with many titles of doubtful
taste and quality.   It seemed as though the young woman
was leaning over backwards to show how modern and broad-
minded she was; as though she *dared* not suggest a Hardy,
an Austen, a Bronte, a George Eliot, or even a C.P. Snow
or an Anthony Powell.

Susan Hill, in a recent review of a new book by Dame
Helen Gardner, quoted her as saying that the bodies that
prepare literary syllabuses these days tend to choose modern
works, be they of varying values, on 'the spurious ground
that they "speak directly" to the reader about the world
which he knows and with which he can 'identify', although

many of them may prove to be 'ephemeral'. It does seem a pity that the young should not have a solid basis of literary worth and taste before being let loose amongst the modish and meretricious, when their judgement is more secure.

However, since I set out to talk about memories of youthful reading I must finish by saying how much to be envied are the very young of today: it seems there has never been such a vast quantity and infinite variety at their disposal, the worst being at least harmless, the best comfortably homely or charmingly fantastic, with bold, colourful illustrations. . . . and many of the children and animals delightfully naughty!

Remembering the dull, moral tales of our youth, I wonder how we would have coped with such a plethora of goodies!

CHAPTER VI

"LUPINS" – AT SCHOOL IN HULL

When I was about eight or nine years old, that was more than 75 years ago, I attended for a time a day preparatory school in Yorkshire. It was housed in a suburban mansion, one of several in varying Edwardian styles, standing in a cul-de-sac, which was lined with trees and terminated by the pretty wrought-iron gates of a park.

All very pleasant and superior, no doubt, but what still looms darkly in my mind is the school's high greybrick tower of menacing aspect. It contained empty-looking windows, and therefore, presumably, rooms; but this mysterious region was out-of-bounds to the pupils, and we often wondered if Very Naughty Girls were incarcerated there as a punishment.

The school uniform was dark navy: a pleated gym-slip of standard design, and a coat . . heavy wool reefer-cloth in winter, and gabardine in summer; and in all seasons we wore black woollen stockings, square shoes or boots, and a hard yellow straw boater, known as a 'cady', with a black peter-sham band adorned with the school badge.

The school was small; but snobbish, scholarly, and strict. The cane was not unknown, but more common punishments were 'lines' or detention. How the latter operated I cannot imagine, since no child was allowed to leave the premises unless seen to be collected by an approved parent or guardian. Perhaps the fond mothers entered the building and endured detention along with their erring offspring, or perhaps they paraded in the Park until the penal session was over.

I remember well one of our text-books; "An Outline of British History", which dealt with all matters political and military from Boadicea to the Boer War. Outline indeed! It was thick, closely printed in small type, contained no illustrations, and was much given to such phrases as . . "the era of unchallengeable chartered liberty and vested interest, the greatest charter of all" . . and . . "the Barons, having no idea of parliamentary institutions, could only devise the most clumsy means to enforce the treaty they had wrung from the

momentary need of their shifty and able adversary . . " . .
Ordinary people and everyday happenings apparently did not
exist in 'history'; the book was dismally boring, and we had
to learn large chunks of it by heart.

Despite its total unattractiveness, I remember taking a
certain pride and satisfaction in it.

We moved several times in my childhood, and I attended
school in various places . . Preston, Glasgow, Hull, Newcastle-
on-Tyne, Manchester, Stockton-on-Tees, Buckingham. . and,
with a certain superior air I took the heavy tome with me
when I moved from the Hull school back to the little school
in Preston, and showed it to my new form-mistress. I shall
never forget the feeling of personal shame, not to say deep
guilt, with which I listened, red-faced, and in tears, to her
scathing words of criticism "*Most* unreadable . . . . a wholly
unsatisfactory book for children!. . misguided choice . . .
ruining a child's view of history!" and so on. Both she and I
(then eight years old) seemed to be under the illusion that I
personally had chosen the offending book.

The Great Australian Bight and the Great Barrier Reef
spanned our horizon. The natural resources of Africa were
glued to a large cardboard wall-map in symbolic form: a
brass paper-clip indicated the presence of gold; a fragment of
glass betokened diamonds; a morsel of coal, and sundry
seeds, and chips of teak and other timbers, denoted a variety
of exports.

Straits, isthmuses, and watersheds were driven home by
means of representations in clay and sand.

The commoner wild flowers were thoroughly dissected
and their parts minutely copied into Nature drawing-books.
The Birds and the Bees were adequately dealt with . . the
existence of male and female duly noted; we even reached . .
near thing . . stamens, stigma and pollen . . but *no* further.

The Headmistress I recall all too clearly. She seemed
to be about eighty; she had a whalebone waist, and wore
rimless eyeglasses, or 'pince-nez', which looked upon us, all
askew, with a terrifying glint.

My form-mistress, however, cast a kindly glance upon
me every now and then; and I upon her. I adopted the
habit of placing, each week, a bunch of flowers upon her
desk, much in the same spirit as the ancient Greeks laid
oblations in their shrines to buy off the wrath of the gods.

Once, on the appropriate day, I forgot this offering;
but as our home was fairly near the school, I decided I had
time to run back. From the garden I grabbed two ragged
fistfuls of extremely tall lupins; and with this huge purple
swathe drooping from óne arm, and my heavy school-bag

bumbling from the other, I made off for school again in fearful haste.

It was the rule for pupils to enter by the main front door; the tradesman's entrance was reserved for the Second Mistress's bicycle. The hallway was long and wide; the Assembly Hall, made, I imagine, from the merging of two rather grand reception rooms, opened off it not far from the front door. It was the custom for the girls to assemble in some nether region, thence to march smartly, two by two, along this hallway into Assembly for daily Prayers and Notices.

There were no girls in the road that morning; none in the garden, none on the front step. The great front door was ominously shut.

I opened it slowly, and beheld with horror the two leading girls, monitors, flanked by a mistress, already marching briskly towards me down the long hall. I had no option but to stand my ground defenceless, raked by sixty pairs of eyes, some creasing with incipient giggles, some wide with sympathetic apprehension; and others, those of monitors and staff, full of stern disapproval. I tried to hide my crimson face behind my unfortunate bouquet, which by now was assuming the proportions of the huge lime-tree at the front gate.

Finally, came the Headmistress. As the last two girls entered the hall she paused, looked down upon me, and said, "Margery, you are late! An explanation will be due after Assembly. Meanwhile, kindly walk into the hall, in front of me, *just as you are!*"

'Just as I was!' (without one plea) In front of her! In front of everyone! In my outdoor clothes! With my ridiculous bundle of wilting and broken flora! Oh no! I knew this was intended as a punishment of exquisite torture. I also knew it was one of those occasions when my legs would refuse to do what my brain told me must be done.

I turned, swept past the Headmistress down the long hall, and sought refuge in the cloakroom, where I sank limply onto a boot-locker, and awaited retribution.

There followed several minutes of dreadful silence. Then without more disturbance, came the firm closing of the Assembly Hall door, and the rising strains of "Another day begun; Lord grant us grace that we-e". . Many hours seemed to pass; then a monitor appeared. I was to go to the Headmistress's desk in the Hall, now, at once!

Flinging down most of my bundle I followed her through the door, down the Hall, between staring rows of pupils; miserably conscious of my clumping outdoor shoes, my bulging bag still swinging from my shoulder, my tilted 'cady' with its perished elastic knotted into a grey twizzle under one cheek . . and a partially deflowered length of greenery still clutched in one sweating palm.

I stood before the terrible throne at the head of the Hall. "Why were you late?" The spectacles glittered at me. I tried to explain about the flowers, unconsciously brandishing the single wilting specimen under her nose, as though in evidence for the defence.

"Much, much worse than your lateness, you have been disobedient to me! Why did you not precede me into the Hall as directed?" This time I was speechless, and once again could only raise the rumpled bloom in mute explanation and entreaty.

I forget what form of punishment was selected for me, but what ever it was it could not have been a worse ordeal than what went before. And if I had to write out five hundred times "I must not be disobedient", those lines, too, have faded into the mists of time.

But I can never see a bed or spray of lupins without powerful recollections of that distressing incident, and especially of shame at my moral cowardice.

Perhaps the lupins are 'en rapport' with me in this matter, for they never will grow in my garden.

CHAPTER VII

GOING TO THE MOTION PICTURES

When I was approaching eight years old a friend of my mother's asked if she might take me, along with her own small daughter, to see one of those new-fangled motion pictures. On health and moral gounds my mother was obviously very dubious, but finally decided that her friend's judgment could not be so very wrong.

I have three clear memories of this exciting outing. First, the most vivid of all, the girl in this amazing moving photograph who clung with her fingers to an outside window-sill while fire raged all about her. She was rescued only when the hem of her dress seemed actually to catch alight.

Secondly, the antics of the lady pianist during this breath-taking episode could not be ignored. She sat just below the screen, her hands ranging madly up and down the keys, during which her head kept bobbing up and obliterating the captions at the bottom of the screen. At the final moment of deliverance she nearly cleaved the instrument in half with her crashing chords. Finally, eating between meals being strictly forbidden, I had the guilty pleasure of buying sweets from a little stall and eating them during the performance.

It was a long time before I visited again such an exciting show, but meanwhile, as the industry developed, modest little picture-houses sprang up, each having a manager whose personal choice built up the programme. They were usually gentlemanly and friendly, and always in evidence in the front foyer to receive compliments or complaints, and to see everyone safely off the premises.

Gradually a fairly standard programme became established: the Pathe Gazette News . . . . mostly domestic, because there was not the means of getting foreign news quickly enough . . . a Nature film, a comic, and the main feature, usually either highly sentimental or melodramatic. Some of the nature films were well advanced in technique, and I particularly remember a series produced by one Margery Field, which, with the use of fast cameras produced wonderful pictures of buds slowly opening, birds and insects in flight, and so on.　　While the main features were totally lacking in reality, they were mostly highly moral and harmless to the young . . . "Is it *nice*?" my mother used to ask.

The trite situations, the obligatory happy endings, and the totally impossible 'dangers' made it unlikely that they made much impression on anyone's mind.　　The exciting serials, designed to draw their weekly audiences, usually had a girl tied to a railway line before an oncoming train, the camera whisking from girl to train and back again repeatedly until the rescue was greeted by roars and stamping from the audience.　　Or a villain was cornered on a high roof, or in mortal danger from fire or water.　　Many people will remember "The Perils of Pauline" or "The Exploits of Elaine".

The jerky action, the mouthed words with dubbed captions badly synchronised, did not call for well-constructed plots or stories with any substance; and so far no one had thought of adapting for the screen good plays or books.

Action being the keynote of the motion picture or 'animated photograph', comedy of the banana-skin variety comprised the bulk of the comic programmes.　　Where meaningful dialogue was stilted or lacking altogether, it was obvious that action, and the most exaggerated at that, captured the picture audiences, and very cleverly staged and photographed these sequences were.　　The genre produced many stars of the silent screen:　the Keynote Cops, Laurel and Hardy, Buster Keaton and, of course, the inimitable Charlie Chaplin.　　His skilful acting, and the basic appeal of the 'sad clown', the pathetic little failure in life, raised him above all others.　　In the case of Harold Lloyd, another favourite comic, clever trick photography was the chief ingredient in the success of his hair-raising adventures.

As children, we never suffered the suspense of the weekly serial, as my mother regarded a regular indulgence in any form of outside entertainment as evidence of empty minds.　　The hordes of children, unaccompanied by adults, streaming out from the tuppenies and fourpennies of the Saturday matinee, all chewing sweets moreover, earned her deepest disapproval, as self-indulgent, extravagent, and mind-weakening.　　Commercial entertainment of any kind should be reserved as a very special treat.

And so, on Boxing Day, we were allowed to visit the local suburban cinema for the special children's matinee, with the requisite News, Comic, Nature Film, and a specially chosen main feature, usually a fairy story such as "Where the Rainbow Ends".

Occasionally, when we were older, an extra visit was permitted when something highly recommended and mind-improving was featured. I shall never forget "The Great White Silence", the re-enacted story of Scott's expedition to the South Pole. A string trio accompanied this picture, and whenever I hear Schubert's "Unfinished Symphony" I think of the heart-rending scene where Scott's friend, Captain Oates, suffering severely from frost-bite, said, "I am going out for a few minutes", and stumbling forth into the blizzard lay down in the snow to freeze to death. They knew, as he did, that he could walk no further, and nothing could be done about it.

With the coming of the great American epics, and finally of the 'talkies', the modest little picture-houses gave way to the monster cinema palaces, and at the heyday of British Films . . . including, among others, the spate of Ealing Comedies, so charming, so simple-minded . . . . every town had its vast gilded, plush-seated, and elaborately lighted auditoria, its Granadas, Imperials, Savoys, Alhambras and Olympias. The splendour of these buildings was more than skin-deep, it marked an exceptional era in the entertainment world, and many of them, so redolent of a past age, are preserved as listed buildings.

A re-showing of the "Golden Oldies" on television demonstrates the innocent charm and humour of the British films, and the magnificent scenic effects and vivid action of the Hollywood products. The growth of the American film industry with its lavish musicals, splendid Westerns and spectacular biblical epics began to fill our cinemas. They would have had nothing to learn from modern techniques, for their skills and trick photography in gigantic scenarios and the handling of huge crowd scenes made them unique in entertainment; and the fact that they could rival without swamping the British industry was due to their total contrast to the quiet domestic humour of the British film.

The glycerine tears of Edna Best demonstrates the superficiality of the acting: a modern actress on film or television can become so involved that real tears and uncontrollable facial muscles are far more moving than, say, Elizabeth Taylor's ham acting of emotional scenes.

Such a flourishing industry naturally produced its stars, though they were hardly then known as such; and in an age when matinees of both cinema and theatre could draw their audiences of leisured ladies, there had to be box-office celebrities . . . the handsome hero, the beauteous heroine.

An outstanding one of the former was Owen Nares, he of the dimpled chin, the Greek profile, the corrugated hair.

The female draw of that period was Edna Best, a charming young woman with large soulful eyes, an oval face, tender mouth, and smooth, shining hair, and who appeared, as far as black-and-white photography disclosed, to be a blue-eyed blonde; and what is more, in my mother's opinion, a *'lady'*! Delicate love affairs between these two made young wives nearly swoon in their red plush stalls.

I remember my mother being tempted to treat herself to a Saturday matinee featuring this romantic pair. I, being about nine or ten years old, had perforce to be taken along. . I am sure against her better judgment . . . there presumably being no one available to mind me. I seem to remember the story being one of mild marital misunderstanding, but the sequence depicting the happy reunion was one that puzzled me greatly. Edna Best was observed sitting by the fire knitting a pair of tiny bootees, whereupon Owen Nares, glowing with rapturous surprise, his mouth and eyes performing wonders of expression, fell on his knees and embraced her shoulders, fondling the little sock, and gazing admiringly into her tearful eyes.

Now I knew exactly what these tiny socks meant, and sensed at once my mother edging away from me, both mentally and physically, lest I should ask awkward questions. But by now I had learnt from a well-informed school-friend that a husband and wife had to do something special together in order to bring about the arrival of a baby. We didn't know exactly what it was, and I don't remember that we were particularly interested, but the romantic knitting scene brought confusion to my mind. If the lady was expecting a baby to arrive, then they must have done together whatever it was they were required to do. Why, therefore, had she to *tell* her husband what he must have known already? Why was he so overtaken with joyous surprise?

As we emerged from the smokey, stuffy picture-house, I considered long and hard whether to ask my mother to elucidate this problem, but decided against it, largely because I knew what the response would be. "Oh, what a silly picture . . such rubbish . . . forget it! Now, let us hurry for our tram-car!"

The advent of the wide three-D film brought the excitement of seeming audience-participation in the action; but even they have not been able to gain huge popularity against the lure of the small comfortable screen at home. Hence the closing-down of most town cinemas, and the demise of the British Film Industry as we knew it.

I think this is a sad loss to society, and though 'going to the pictures' was never a very formative influence in *our* lives, the screen purveyed information, entertainment, and 'good clean fun': an excursion and a treat which offered something quite different from the present-day absorption in the 'Box' in our own homes.

I remember going one afternoon on a school outing to the local Picture House to see a "Nature" film, and was allowed to walk back from the assembly point with a little friend. Nearing her home we saw a ladder propped at the upper window of a house - probably a window-cleaner's. "Do you know", she said, "if a man climbs up a ladder into a lady's window at night she is always ill next morning?" "Oh, is she?" I said. "And did you know that ladies are often ill and have to go to bed just when a baby's coming? *I* know, because my friend next door had a little brother, and her mother was still in bed when the baby came to her. Wasn't it a pity?" And with that we resumed the much more engrossing topic of how awful our parents were.

CHAPTER VIII

ON BOOKS AND PEOPLE IN TRANSIT

Long ago I used to travel daily on a long, narrow, single-decker tram-car, known as the caterpillar. Each of its twin trolleys was bound round with a sort of coarse black insulating-tape, and the little wheels at the top, when they passed over a junction in the overhead cables, emitted a firework display of electric sparks. Its bogey-wheels seemed peculiarly unsuited to the track, or vice versa, since the journey was accompanied by a cacophany of groanings, squeakings and clankings that made speech, and even thought, impossible.

The seating consisted of a long bench down each side, for the uncomfortable accommodation of the maximum number of passengers. If a new fare stared long and wistfully enough at a small gap, the others would 'nudge up a bit' and resentfully allow the newcomer to wedge in.

I found myself once so placed between two young women who, despite the metallic uproar above and below, were deeply immersed in novels of high romance, with garish dust-covers depicting palms and sheiks and sand and dark faces, and jewelled trousers and blue distances.

On my right, Chapter IV began, "Diana noticed a movement under the bananas. It was her husband", which conjured amusing visions of a midgetty little man popping out of the fruit bowl. On my left, I read something like, "she saw the shimmering Karoo stretching for untold miles around her, while a hot breeze from the flaming sunset fanned her cheeks." I guessed them to be by Ethel M. Dell, or Berta Ruck, or Ruby M. Ayres. Heady stuff. . . even for those days.

Observing reading-matter on trains is always interesting. Tattered students, especially on Oxford trains, always seem to be wrestling with theses; business men attend raptly to reports or columns of figures. Serious cross-word puzzlers are always male, and sitting in corner seats. When they stare out over the passing scene, biro poised, and a glazed look in the eye, it means they are grappling intensely for the right word. I itch to ask for the clue, not because I think I would be cleverer than the would-be solver, but two minds working together tend to stimulate thought; like two shafts of 'lateral thinking' as it were, impinging on a point and illuminating it.

I remember a Mr. Pooter-like gentleman, darkly dressed, with black bowler, toothbrush moustache, and wobbly pince-nez, holding vertically aloft before his eyes Housman's "A Shropshire Lad". Since he turned over but one page between London and Wolverhampton, and occasionally went into a sort of trance, I assumed he was trying to commit some lines to memory. He looked singularly unpoetic, though, more like an undertaker.

Disembarking passengers seldom leave newspapers of worth behind them; they are too expensive. But vacant seats are often draped with the "Sun" or "Star", casually open at nudes or footballers, garnished with empty chip-bags and broken plastic cups.

In the early days of motor-cars, road travel and reading did not accord; too much jolting, bouncing and dust. Only picnics or break-downs afforded the chance of a good read. I never drove any but second-hand cars, all disastrously unreliable; and I had only two methods of dealing with emergencies, one or other of which usually worked. One was to raise the hinged side of the bonnet and poke at something inside with a hairpin. The other was to sit by the roadside looking unspeakably pathetic, when a kind passing motorist would draw up and offer aid.

A friend of mine had bought a stone cottage in a bleak village in the Peak District of Derbyshire, and there she and her brother held weekend parties which were scenes of hilarious innocent merriment from start to finish. I drove out there alone rather late one night, and my car chose "to cease upon the midnight with no pain", and, upon a lonely hill road. Neither hairpins nor passing motorists . . . the latter conspicuous by their absence. . . could solve its problems.

There was nothing for it but to leave the car and set out to walk. This I did with sleeping-baggage in one hand, and in the other a string bag containing "Villette", "A la Recherche du Temps Perdus", and an aluminium hot-water-bottle full of cold cocoa. Thus accoutred, I landed on my friend's door-step at 2 a.m. She was not in the least surprised; and next morning the boys went out, relay-cycling, and managed to bring in the ailing car.

And talking of bicycles and books, I did once see a Cambridge under-graduate wobbling along, one hand on handlebar, the other holding aloft an open book. I used to

38

carry First World War Poets in the battered saddlebag of my ancient bike . . . literally held together with string. . . as I pedalled along leafy Buckinghamshire lanes, or in the beautiful beechwoods of the Chilterns. Then sat munching sandwiches with my "book of verses underneath a bough", but "none beside me in the wilderness". In those days, lone females wandering in woodlands ran no risk of being assaulted, done in, and buried in shallow graves.

Ships' libraries were always fascinating, and exemplified the shipping line's estimation of the taste of Passengers Classes I, II and III. There were no package tours in those days; and I found that, cruising alone, one made more acquaintances and had more fun than when setting out with a companion. Meeting in the library was often the start of a cruise friendship: I remember a young lawyer with whom I had terribly serious discussions about such books as Dunne's "Experiment with Time", and the essays of A.C. Benson ("The thread of Gold"), or William James' "The Varieties of Religious Experience", and Einstein's "Theory of Relativity".

Nevertheless, we gathered a jolly crowd together, and had enormous fun organising Fancy Dress Dances for which the rig-outs had to be devised on the spot and pillaged from local sources, such as the sheets off the bunks, or the tasselled velvet bands from the saloon curtains. The ship was "The City of Nagpur" of Ellerman Line, a splendid gleaming white vessel, on which all the stewards were Lascars and wore turbans, white trousers, and long white coats with brilliant cummerbunds into which were thrust sheathed daggers. Very exciting indeed; and they often conspired with us by lending us their more colourful accessories.

One evening we ran into a Force 8 gale; passengers could not move without being buffeted into walls and furniture. At dinner, one by one, *not* staying to fold their tents (napkins) like the Arabs, they silently stole away, I unhappily among them. In the midst of my misery came a knock at my cabin door, and my friend called, "Come on out and join the crowd, we're all going up front!" "Can't", I wailed, "I'm awfully ill."

"We'll soon see to that", he said, coming in. He went away and came back with a full tumbler of what he said was 'neat' brandy. Wholly unaccustomed to handling strong liquor, I knocked it back in three or four gulps, much as a perspiring tennis addict might sink a lemon barley. The results were spectacular. He sat on my bunk and watched with interest. "Now", he said triumphantly, "*Now* you'll feel better! Wash your face, put on all the coats you've got, and come on up". I did, and we all went up into the prow, holding onto each other and anything else we could clutch. The bows alternately rose up to the stars, and sank into watery valleys, and at each heave, we were drenched with great swooshes of spray and sheets of 'green water'. I never felt so invigorated in all my life. . . "Just imagine staying alone in my bunk being seasick and missing all this fun!" I thought. Which shows what mind can do over matter.

It calmed the next day, and there was a formal dance on the upper after-deck, with fairy lights and a string orchestra. The girls all pressed their dresses beforehand in the ironing-room. We wore long diaphanous gowns with lots of gussets and floating panels, and long ear-rings; and the more daring among us smoked cigarettes in long ivory or ebony holders. very Michael Arlen.

The moon and stars shone brightly as we swayed on the sloping decks to the strains of "Three O'Clock in the Morning", and I thought I would never again know anything so romantic and glamorous.

There was a lovely golden girl, dressed all in white chiffon on that occasion. I had often noticed her: she was travelling with her parents, and we became acquainted. She seemed to me a pure Pre-Raphaelite type; like a less intense version of Rossetti's "The Blessed Damozel", or a more smiling "Astarte Syriaca", or "Proserpine". I asked my lawyer friend if he agreed, and he confessed disappointingly that he had never even noticed her. This was quickly remedied; and thereafter he became very friendly with the family; and told me that after the cruise he was going back home with them for a visit. He thanked me ardently for drawing his attention to her: it was a case of noticing, becoming interested, then friendly, thence to headlong fall into love! Now, wasn't that interesting? I felt quite a matchmaker, and felt sure they would marry some day.

But the return journey had its adventures too. We were to call in at Oslo, but the "City of Nagpur" was a big ship and had to stand off, anchored outside the bay. Those passengers wishing to take a trip into the mountains, or a cruise in small boats round the innumerable little wooded islands, had to go ashore in a tender. On our return to the ship we were run down by a huge cargo vessel laden with timber, I was near the starboard rail, and watched with astonishment the inexorable approach of its towering black bows. One man started to jump over the rail, but was restrained. We were rammed amidships, and I was flung down the deck and brought up painfully against a bulkhead;

but not too dazed to notice the port rail sliding gently beneath the water. "So, this is it", thought I.

In slow seconds the tender miraculously righted itself, and everyone sat or lay about looking rather pale or mopping up tears of relief. A rating said, "There wouldn't have been an earthly if we'd gone down. We'd have been sucked right under the bows of that b. . . .".

Still afloat, we 'limped back', to use the current but wholly inappropriate expression, to the mother ship. Some of us had to visit the doctor, a Scot, as all ships' doctors seemed to be. While he was dressing my injured arm, he asked, "Do you like sailing? How about coming and helping me crew my boat? I've got nieces and nephews coming but I'm one crew short. You'd soon learn the ropes." He told me that there was a model of his yacht in a shop-window in Bond Street, if I cared to have a look at it; he explained where it was, but not *why*. The next time I was in London I found it, sure enough; it looked beautiful, in full sail, and I gazed longingly upon it.

Soon after I had a letter saying they were sailing north from Oban at such-and such a time, where to meet, what clothes to wear, and so on. My father took a dim view of the whole affair, and thought it fishy in the extreme. *I* didn't think so, but I was strictly forbidden to accept the invitation. So there was a good adventure holiday missed!

However, there were others, including a trip in a Fyffe's Banana Boat to the Mediterranean and North Africa, when we spent a day at Gibraltar and a longer sojourn at Casablanca, from where we visited Marrakesh where Mr. Winston Churchill used to sit and paint. How thrilling it was to see real camels and real palm-trees silhouetted black against a burning sunset!

A more modest cruise was on a Macbrayne's cargo coaster up the west coast of Scotland. It carried to each small port barrels of beer and timber, corrugated iron sheeting, zinc bath-tubs, and sheep; and all the men engaged in the operations spoke in Gaelic.

They took only twelve passengers, and the one long saloon-cum-dining room was flanked by the cabins and various toilet arrangements. I remember one passenger who always seemed to get her timing wrong. As soon as we were all seated for dinner, she emerged from her cabin in the bows wearing a flowing silk gown decorated with buttercups, and a floppy bath-cap. Carrying her towels and an enormous bath-sponge, she squeezed behind the diners' chairs down to a bathroom in the stern end. The emergence of Miss Buttercup was one of the nightly amusements.

41

Once when we were out in more open sea, passing the Point of Ardna-murchan, I think it was, the boat bounced, vibrated and juddered, and all liquids on the table danced out of their containers. Miss B's staggering passage from the bathroom was watched with interest. At one point she lurched into a diner's chair, and her huge sponge flew into his prunes and custard.

I once sailed in a small boat to the Isle of Barra, and stayed there in a little 'black house'. A couple from St. Ives were holidaying there and we toured the island together in a funny old horse-drawn cart. Compton Mackenzie's house, where he kept his vast collection of gramophone records, was one of the places we visited. It stood on a long, narrow spit of land, where a thin green film of tide spread in over the sand on one side, and on the other great Atlantic breakers rolled in over a stony shore.

I remember another bumpy voyage, though in very different circumstances. We were sailing at midnight from Patras down the Gulf of Corinth. The night was black, but the waves, under the ship's lights, were a deep luminous blue, with white crests. The coach on which we were touring, was parked, untethered, on a lower deck; and at frequent intervals, it jumped bodily into the air, landing on its eight wheels with a tremendous thump.

We all felt weary and a little queasy, when a schoolmaster in the party suddenly conducted us, with waving arms, into singing "Clementine", "Riding down from Bangor", and other favourites from the "Scottish Students' Song Book." We moved on to Cecil Sharp's arrangements, such as "The Water of Tyne", "O, Waly, Waly", "Strawberry Fair", "Green Broom" and sea-shanties . . "Rio Grande", and "Bobby Shaftoe". More and more joined in, and our voices rang round the jolting decks, while Greek passengers stared with astonished interest at such uninhibited behaviour on the part of the British. Books again. . . but of a different kind; calling to mind their contents, and rendering them with gusto, heartened and cheered a rather eerie voyage.

Meanwhile the couple met on Barra had invited me to spend a holiday with them in Cornwall the following summer. His mother was also staying there, and she was the most beautiful *old* lady I had ever seen. Her silver-white hair surmounted a smooth, oval pink-and-white face. . . unaided by make-up of course. . . and her large violet eyes were eloquent with an amused and tender look of interest and concern. Her low, soft voice seemed to express a totally selfless and loving sympathy with the whole of mankind. There was nothing mawkish or insincere about all this sweetness and gentle charm. She looked as though she could be as firm as a rock over matters that she thought important; and I still carry with me the memory of her absolute beauty of face, voice and manner. What a mother-in-law to be proud of!

And talking of beauty being more than skin-deep, I remember too an occasion, much later in life, when in the Second World War, among other occupations, I did some lecturing to "Wrens" at Inshore Naval Establishments, though I can't think how or why this came about.

The speakers always dined with officers before taking to the rostrum; and on one occasion I happened to have on my right hand a Wren officer of high rank. She was impeccably uniformed, but with the most unfortunate complexion, sallow, and disfigured with batches of angry red spots. But she had the utmost charm of manner, and the most sprightly and delightful conversation. A prosperous-looking Armenian gentleman with an unpronounceable name. . . I can't think what *he* was lecturing about. . . was sitting opposite her, and was clearly enchanted. To use a cliche, her voice and manner held one spellbound, and she made the evening memorable, obviously to him, as to me. I often wondered if *they* met again, and ultimately married.

I have wandered far from the subject of books and reading-matter, so will return to them in the context again of a rail journey. To a particular one from Manchester to Euston, where I had taken the only vacant seat, which happened to be next to a young man who was laughing aloud at intervals over a copy of "Punch". I could not forbear glancing sideways at the drawings, and soon he politely moved the paper over in my direction. We laughed together at the jokes, thence to the reading-matter, and finally to a conversation which lasted animatedly over the whole too-short journey to London.

"When are you returning?" he asked. "Oh, some time Sunday evening, I expect. I have to be at work on Monday morning." We said thanks for a jolly journey, and goodbye.

Sitting on my return train, just before departure, I saw his face at the window. He entered and sat down with me. "I've walked the length of the train, looking in at every window," he said. "But how did you know I'd be on this train?" "It seemed the obviously convenient one, so I came along," he said.

We talked all the way back, without aid of "Punch", about every subject under the sun. At Piccadilly Station, Manchester, he said, "Would you like some tea?" "I'd love it." He took me to the Queen's Hotel, then one of Manchester's most exclusive, with a palm court and string orchestra for thes dansants. He ordered a delicious tea; and talked about his work and life, and affectionately about his wife and children.

He never asked my name, nor I his. "I must go now", I said, and thanked him for the tea and two pleasant journeys, and said goodbye. To have exchanged addresses, murmured something about 'meeting again', or "Do you often travel to London?" would have spoilt it all. It was an entertaining interlude, and complete. Finis.

"Your train was very late," said my mother. "No, it wasn't," I said "I've been having tea at the Queen's with a perfectly strange young man. Explanations required; but no proper *understanding*, I thought!

Harking back on past events is supposed to be a sign of approaching senility, rather a waste of time; and dreadfully boring to all but the most sympathetic and polite of the young. But it can be fun.

With many divergencies into other memories, so much for the adventures and consequences of interesting oneself in books and reading en voyage.

CHAPTER IX

OF LAUNDRY-TUBS AND THINGS

Nothing makes one feel so old, or such a member of a past generation, as seeing displayed, as antiques, the ordinary domestic objects of one's youth.

I remember standing before a little shop called "Domestic Bygones" in the village of Stow-on-the-Wold and exclaiming at the articles of 'historic interest' that were in common daily use in my mother's wash-house and kitchen. As for implements and vessels seen in my grandmother's house, they were really rare and valuable pieces.

The same sort of domestic ware, but on a larger scale, can be seen in the kitchen regions of some of the stately homes of Britain. Drumlanrig Castle in Dumffriesshire comes to mind; the famously restored Erddig in Clwyd, Hartlebury Castle in Worcestershire, the White House at Aston Munslow in Shropshire; Brighton Pavilion, and many others. I have even seen flat-irons displayed as ornaments on the oak mantel of a modernised cottage.

The feeling of rather resentful, sad familiarity with such bygones is intensified for me by my having struggled and fought with them for a precious three years of my life. Doomed, under parental duress, to a three-year course in what was then known as domestic science, I had ample opportunity to wield what were to me these implements of torture. When I see them resurrected in shops and museums I can picture vividly the great rooms of that "House of Correction", particularly the laundry-rooms; and with that vision I experience something like the sentiments that Emily Bronte expressed in her woeful verses:

"Oh, dreadful is the check, intense the agony
When the ear begins to hear and the eye begins to see;
When the pulse begins to throb, the brain to think again;
The soul to feel the flesh, and the flesh to feel the
                                                    chain."

The flesh and the spirit certainly felt the chain, and the iron, on many occasions.

Well, concerning that laundrywork, there were two enormous rooms each fitted along one end with a series of

45

heavy wooden troughs, rather like the hay-boxes in stables. In each trough was a zinc rubbing-board, (the things some 'groups' now use to make 'music' with) and a posser, a large copper bell with holes in its sides and a stout wooden handle, which washed, by suction, woollens and delicate materials. To each two troughs was assigned a large wooden tub, like a cooper's beer keg, each furnished with a dollypeg. This was like a four-legged milking-stool, with a strong upright and crossbar, which was plunged into the sudsy washing in the tub and alternately lifted and twisted . . . plunge, twist right, plunge, twist left . . . a movement calculated to develop biceps and bust to an alarming degree. In one corner stood the bricked-in boiler where the 'whites' were required to bubble furiously for at least twenty minutes, the coke fire being stoked from time to time through a little iron door at the base.

In another corner stood a strange iron pagoda with faceted sides against which were heated the flat-irons, and which grew red-hot when over-stoked with coke. Some of the facets were concave to take the small polishing-irons with which we produced the blue-white glacial surfaces of men's stiff collars and dress-shirts. Standing nearby was a large wooden trough of powdered bathbrick. The irons, having been spat upon to test the heat by the degree of 'sizzle' produced, were well rubbed in this and cleaned with a coarse duster. They were then polished with a pure white testing-cloth before going into action on the complicated apparel or napery. This lay, duly sprinkled with water after drying, and tightly rolled to 'spread the moisture'. There was also a special gas-heater for the crimping-tongs with which we had to finish off the frills of pillowslips, aprons, and the staff's elaborate linen caps.

To be really up-to-date the laundry was also furnished with a modern 'mechanical' washing-machine, a huge wooden tub such as men trod grapes in. The wood paddles inside worked by various cog-wheels to a lever at the side which the student pumped desperately to and fro when favoured with the use of this sophisticated appliance.

The centre of the room was occupied by six enormous tables with sycamore wood tops two-and-a-half inches thick, and these had to be scrubbed with a mixture of green soft soap and whiting until their surfaces shone like creamy-grey silk.

Although taught to hang clothes in a correct manner on a line out-of-doors, we had to rely on the iron bars of a huge drying-chamber because a family wash or set of garments had to be aired, displayed, and inspected within one morning's or afternoon's session.

The word 'inspected' brings me swiftly to recollections of our laundry tutor. Can you imagine the teacher of such a humdrum subject looking as she did?. . . . a tall statuesque figure with rod-straight back, silvery hair swept up in a French pleat, her frilled white cap of office like a coronet above it; a face of craggy beauty reminiscent of Sybil Thorndyke in one of her more soulful, heaven-gazing moments in Shaw's "St. Joan." But when anything displeased her, as it frequently did, the eyebrows shot up at the corners, the mouth down, and the eyes became steely slits. Whenever a student was obliged to confess to some misdemeanor she was greeted with, "You did *what!*" in tones like Edith Evans' famous 'handbag' line.

We called her the Duchess, and she was in fact, the doyenne of the more mature members of the staff who set the standard for the College. A group of straight-backed, straight-laced ladies who were indeed ladies in every then known sense of the word, . . . refined, just, stern, high-minded, responsible and efficient to a degree. All of them, and especially the Duchess, had but one standard, and that was . . . perfection. She, in fact, raised laundering to a high art and craft.

The scientific knowledge underlying the materials and cleaning-agents we used was, of course, dealt with by the science tutor, in the chemistry laboratories, but the laundries had their own demonstration theatre, and when the Duchess went on stage there it was a theatrical event indeed, apart from being able to sit down and ease our aching shoulders and fallen arches.

I remember being in favour with the Duchess once, when, in response to a general request to the class for offers of anything rather bizarre, I produced my father's christening gown, which happened to provide every element necessary to show off the finer points of laundering. As was usual it had tiny puffed sleeves edged with fine lace; a tucked bodice, a draw-string in the neck . . . all tapes and ribbons in underwear, however fine, had to be withdrawn, ironed flat, and replaced with a bodkin . . . but in addition to serried rows of tucks round its voluminous hem, it had a widening front panel which consisted of alternate bands of ruching and lace insertion, each about 2 inches wide. The ruching was gathered fully at both sides, and its full effect was brought out by the use of the egg-iron. This was of polished iron about the size of a large duck-egg, mounted on a wooden stand. The egg was heated on a special heater cleaned, polished and mounted, then the ruched sections were passed *over* the iron, so that they ballooned out between the lace. The tiny sleeves also needed treatment by the egg-iron; and the smallest size flat-iron was used for the minute edging. When the Duchess had finished the effect was superb. She called it 'my Henry VIIIth baby gown.'

Another of her magical demonstrations was the cleaning of dark felt hats with a concoction of stewed ivy leaves, finished off with a tossing in bran and a stiff brushing. Light felts were refreshed with Fuller's Earth or dressmaker's chalk. (I might add here that we were taught to clean patent leather shoes with creamy milk, to stiffen old lace in a strong sugar solution; and to brighten dark carpets with ox-gall . . a viscous green fluid which persuaded us that dirty carpets were infinitely preferable).

The washing and ironing of silk ring velvet was another of her acts. But her real tour-de-force . . and I wonder to how many generations of students she performed this one . . . was the dry-cleaning of ostrich feathers, the kind debutantes had to wear in their hair when presented at Court.

But for full effect the Duchess produced, not white feathers, but brilliant orange ones. She waved the delicate fronds dramatically in the air, then laid them reverently on the demonstration table.

All bunsen burners and other naked flames were inspected to see that they were firmly turned off; the huge windows were thrown open. Then entered two 'runners', (the maids who were appointed, two to each practice room, to do the rough work. . . we were always in league with them, and they saved us from many a potential disaster). They each carried a large heavy enamel bowl which they placed in front of the Duchess. She then plunged the feathers deep into the first bowl: an odour of petrol fumes reeked up to the top benches of the theatre. She held up the dripping limp objects for a few seconds, then thrust them into the second bowl. Out came three long streaks of white slime. A moment's breathless pause; then she shook the feathers vigorously, and there they were . . . beautiful, fluffy, fresh and curling! "Ordinary white flour!" she beamed. "Well, the best quality cake flour, of course!"

The Duchess had one glaring fault: she was a terrible snob; and she had her favourites.

One student in our class was a striking character: she was tall with large brown eyes, a large nose, and a deep husky voice. Her hair was cropped very short like a boy's; in contrast to our long hair, which was put up with hair-pins to show we were grown-up. She was a good actress, and played the violin divinely, and so she was God's own gift to our various drama and music societies. Her father owned cotton mills, and was extremely rich; hence, all the articles Miss Cooper brought to wash were of the highest possible quality. Her double-damask table-linen was thick and smooth as hand-laid paper; her pure silk scarves were rich and heavy, and had minutely hand-rolled hems. Her woollens were luxurious and never shrank. The embroidery on her satin underskirts stood out boldly; and her silk stockings, when pressed and folded, fell gracefully into a neat oblong. It was obvious that, with even less than perfect laundering, these articles, when displayed for inspection, must always gain the highest marks.

The Duchess was positively reverent about good napery: table-clothes, even very large ones, had to be impeccably stiff, smooth, and creaseless, and had to be ironed into a four-screen-fold, which gave a proper symmetry when the cloth was spread. Table-napkins had to be in a three-screen fold, each selvedge aligned exactly with the folds, and the end folds precisely together. Show a dog-eared corner, and the offending article was picked up by the Duchess and flung back into the wash-tub.

Of course, Miss C's. high-quality linen simply aligned itself without effort, whilst those of us who had linen with wavy hems had to struggle with repeated dampings and pressings to gain the desired effect.

However, Miss C. was very popular, and there was no malice in the laughter that greeted her final come-uppance. She brought one day, amongst other impressive articles, a pair of high-quality chamois leather gloves for a dry-cleaning session. One of them disappeared. When the 'whites' were removed from their boiling soapy lather, and the latter drained off, there lay at the bottom of the copper a doll's glove, quite perfect in shape, with its tiny fingers and thumb spread out, but absolutely solid, like a lump of stiff yellow jelly. Even the Duchess never let Miss C. forget that.

Meanwhile, my in-favour status, (owing to the Henry VIIIth gown), received a set-back in the course of a practical test.

I drew from a hat the following task: "Launder and display a selection of garments, introducing as many different types of fabric as possible, such as a young lady would take away on a summer holiday."

I included in my selection a nether garment made by myself in the needlework class, a pair of white cotton knickers with the long, wide legs then fashionable. Broad hand-made lace was seamed to the lower hems with minuscule stitches; further up the leg were four bands of narrow handsewn tucks, all parallel to within a millimeter. Above these a rash of embroidery erupted on the outside of each leg. Hedebo-work, it was called, a complicated version of Madeira work, but very open and fragile, and full of traps for the blunt nose of a carelessly-wielded iron. A gathered waist completed the challenge this garment presented.

All gathers had to be poked at with a small no. 2 iron so that each little fold was identical in size.

In the proper manner I dealt with all the fussy bits first. Then I duly polished and sprinkled my iron . . . . spitting on them was not encouraged . . but forgetting to use the final testing-cloth, I placed it firmly on a smoothed-out portion of leg number one . . and withdrew it disclosing a neat brown triangle. Frantic application of all the approved methods of scorch-removal had no effect; I presented the garment unsullied side uppermost; but it was seized, shaken out, examined and displayed to the class. "And *what*, Miss Callis, is that?" Giving a little at the knees, I could only answer weakly, "Yes, they have gone a bit brown, haven't they?" and to my astonished relief, the Duchess threw back her head and laughed heartily. I didn't get many marks though.

About that time, the firm of Courtauld's had invented an imitation silk known as rayon. It was cold, flat and shiny, and when washed behaved in some very peculiar ways. Hence, its properties were the subject of close study in the chemy lab. A too-warm iron placed on a camisole came away with something like treacle spread over its working surface, leaving an iron-shaped vacant space in the garment. Sometimes the material rippled up into a hundred tiny pleats, which never came out. Once, a whole scarf vanished completely in the wash-tub, leaving behind only the straggle of curly thread from its hem.

Oh yes, we had our fun . . and our accidents. A newfangled electric iron once blew up and took the skin off my blackened hand. A gas-oven exploded in my face and deprived me of eyebrows and lashes. And what a fuss was made! I was laid tenderly on the couch in the medical room, covered with blankets, hot milk administered, an ice-pack on my head. I realised later what consternation must have been caused by these mishaps, because of the possibility of parents suing the College.

All the different departments of the College had their hazards . . . and their fun: the hours spent in the chemy labs. . . where, again, I managed to blow up a test-tube in my face . . the art and dress-design, the upholstery, the tailoring and embroidery, the psychology and history of education; the cookery, dietetics, and anatomy. And who could forget the appalling embarrassment of the young science tutor when she had to deliver that *one* awful lecture on "Human Reproduction"?

But I digress from the Duchess and her domain. The time came when I went back, at the age of twenty five, onto the staff of my old college. And because of the prolonged absence of a junior lecturer, I had to teach temporarily . . . of all things . . . laundrywork!

I felt perfectly confident about teaching it . . how young the students all seemed . . . but the Duchess still ruled her kingdom, and conceived it to be her duty to come in and inspect *my* students every so often. Of course, she was really inspecting me, which was not part of her function, and made me feel very nervous. If their work was below the standard she had set, she said little but showed her scorn and displeasure in the usual way. But if their work was excellent, she expressed her congratulations always in the same formula, "Well, you may be their mother, my dear, but don't forget *I'm* their grandmother!"

Looking back, what a terrible waste of time and energy one feels it all was. Why, I can't even buy laundry starch today. "No call for it," I'm told. "Try this. ." a sticky blue fluid sprayed from a bottle, and no use at all. Still, I suppose any art or craft practised to a fanatical degree of excellence makes one's quick housewife's methods so much the better. My husband still demands a white damask table-napkin, and I find myself matching up the corners with fastidious care; and ironing his shirts in the prescribed College manner.

If the Duchess could now see the nylon pillowslips, the little scraps of arty-crafty coloured fibre that pass for 'napery', and *paper* serviettes, she would be revolving in her grave under its crisp, smooth green lawn.

CHAPTER X

WARTIME MEMORIES OF SHROPSHIRE

More than 50 years ago, on a crisp September day, a train from Manchester drew in at Market Drayton station; doors were flung open and streams of bewildered children, arm-banded, labelled and hung with assorted bundles and cardboard gas-mask cases, tumbled from the train and assembled in ragged lines . . and stood waiting.

The sky was bright blue, the sun shining gloriously, and larks singing overhead; but the gloomy clouds of imminent war were hanging over all.

At the head of the platform, a regiment of efficient W.V.S. ladies, the billeting officers, and a host of apprehensive householders stood waiting to receive whatever Fate and the Authorities had sent them in the way of foster-children.

The sorting-out and allotment began at once, but many subdued little groups were still waiting when dusk of the first black-out had descended; and big sisters and brothers, with great resourcefulness and courage, were helping teachers to comfort the smallest tots, most of them overburdened, and all tired, hungry, and frightened by the strangeness of it all.

The year was, of course, 1939, and the occasion the "First Day Evacuation" of the city of Manchester, of some of its 175,000 school children to 'places of safety'.

These places covered wide areas of Lancashire, Cheshire and Shropshire; and for some no doubt good reasons, children from the very poorest industrial parts of Manchester, were chosen for Shropshire's manor-houses, quiet country cottages and flourishing farms. Never in England's history had one half learnt with such brutal suddenness how the other half lived.

This became more depressingly apparent when, on "Second-Day Evacuation", the expectant mothers and those with pre-school age children were brought out and settled with their country hosts.

"None too soon! They have started bombing Warsaw already". These ominous words made many of us feel that, however delightfully and comfortable we were billeted, we had a longing to be at home with our own people in a friendly and familiar environment.

Within a few months, despite the bombing - (still on foreign soil) there started the great trek of 'the mothers who went home'.

Daily warnings of the dangers of returning to the centres of great cities made no impact against the strong desire to get away from a strange environment: from the 'endless fields', the "orrid 'ush of the country', and 'living so near to animals'.

To get away too, from an alien side of behaviour. How many mothers felt bothered and resentful because they were made to bath the baby every day, to teach toddlers to use knife and fork and not to lick the plate; worried when disturbed youngsters quarrelled and shouted before their hosts; because the mothers had to walk two miles to a country shop without a pram. How many of these poor souls did one see, baby in arms and familiar gas-mask hanging from the shoulder, trudging along country lanes looking lost and lonely.

An expectant mother, billeted with her two youngsters at a prosperous farm amazed and angered the hard-working farmer's wife by her habit of lying in bed late into the morning smoking cigarettes, neglecting her children, living almost exclusively out of tins, and tossing into her hostess's ash-bins half-used cans of beans, spam and condensed milk.

Many of these town children were disgusted at the sight of raw egg-white, or rabbits being jointed, hens plucked and cows milked. Most of the mothers, billeted at the very source of country produce could not overcome their repulsion, bred of ignorance and deprivation, at the idea of using foods obtained direct from the farm.

The sharing of kitchens by such disparate housewives could not fail to be a source of almost murderous neuroses before this year of the 'phoney war' had dragged itself to a despondent and nerve-racked end.

Meanwhile, children sent away without their parents began to receive week-end visits from them. The authorities very properly defrayed the expense of a minimum number of visits. Many parents took advantage of this arrangement not only to see their children, but to get a brief trip into the country and away from the threat of bombing.

I can still see one mother, designated as mentally retarded, sitting on the school steps clutching her two (officially 'neglected') children, indiscriminately attacking them with kisses, tears, and blows . . . the latter, because they 'did not want to come home with her'. Small wonder that the confused and bewildered mites never settled, and one heard repeatedly from the lips of teachers and foster-mothers: "We could manage the children perfectly well without the parents . . if only they wouldn't keep coming and unsettling them!"

Children housed in communities with their own teachers, such as "Special School" for handicapped ones put in residence en bloc in a large country hall, fared better in most ways than those enduring the box-and-cox sharing of cramped premises in village schools. One Lady of the Manor, whose young children attended the village school, took as many waifs as she could cram into her large house. Of course they caused the school to bulge at the seams, and the local children looked upon their new classmates as creatures from Mars. They must have been astonished at their tales of grimey streets of back-to-back houses with one water-closet to every four dwellings, and one cold tap for the whole street.

Nevertheless, loving care and attention was lavished upon them by their foster-mother; and I often saw her, in wet weather wearing an old mac and a child's sou'wester perched on top of a bulgeing woollen cap, trudging down the lanes with a pramful . . a delightfully shabby old pram . . of 'mixed infants', with a few more trotting at her side, and much laughter mingling with the raw northern accents.

In more 'feudal' areas, elementary school-teachers were classed socially as servants, and were often housed in hastily-converted attics or even stables. I well remember the kind of Christmas party presented to the children by their well-meaning hosts in some of these communal billets . . tin plates of stodge set in rows on trestle tables, which would have rivalled any Dickensian scene. I saw Manchester teachers nearly weeping with sympathy and exasperation at the disappointment of their poor little charges, who were accustomed to the most lavish and delightful Christmas parties prepared by the joint effort of dedicated teachers and co-operative parents in their own 'slum' schools.

Another memory was of the lady with the chip on her shoulder who had firmly decided that all her tribulations were caused not by Hitler, but by the Manchester L.E.A., who had *no right* to upset her neatly disciplined village school. And so she set out with quiet determination to make life as unpleasant as possible for every child and teacher from those barbarous foreign parts.

"If only she'd lose her temper sometimes, or have a good cry! It's just the quiet smiling way she obstructs every effort at co-operation that gets me down!" said one Manchester teacher after another. I did my best to make truces in these wars of nerves, but often found myself too shaky to drive my car after a session with this composed but bitterly hostile lady. Of course everyone felt sympathy for her and those in like position, but how strangely this unique situation brought out the depths, pleasant and unpleasant, of people's natures. The village and the school are still there looking exactly the same, and I often wonder what became of that unhappy lady.

Then there was the 'fierce Major', retired, a billeting officer, efficient, thorough, kind at heart, doing his duty by his country indeed, but determined that everything would go with military precision under his high command. More tears .. from young untried teachers from city colleges who never dreamed they would be involved in these bizarre rural situations.

One of his duties was to take and introduce me to the Heads of various local schools. He had an ancient but fast car which he drove like Jehu. I was more used to driving in Manchester traffic than negotiating the unknown, narrow, and deep-hedged lanes of Shropshire. The Major flashed like a comet round and through the purlieus of the countryside never once looking behind to see if I was on his tail. I lost him at almost every bend or road junction, but when my guess at his route happened to be right, there he was seething and steaming on the grass verge.

"Can't you damn well keep up with me Miss Whatsyername?" said the gallant Major. "There's a war on! This is no time for dawdling y'know!"

There came a time when the various school officers had to be recalled to Manchester to cope with the growing problem of the mass . . . but unorganised and ill-advised . . . return to the city.

However we asked to make brief return visits to our 'beats' to see how the remnants were faring during the Christmas holidays of a particularly severe winter. On one occasion, foolishly attempting a short cut across country, I boiled in low gear, skidded and slid for miles through hedge-high snow on ice-packed roads, and finally came to rest unscathed at a country hotel in Market Drayton where I stayed for a few days in order to visit the surrounding villages. A musical party one evening at the Vicarage made a pleasant change from these rather dreary pilgrimages.

But the Corbet Arms sported no night-porter, and evidently did not expect returning revellers after midnight. And so it was that the Bishop of Worcester (since retired, but then Vicar of Market Drayton), and the lady Inspector of Schools assisted each other to climb over some spiked railings, when the Vicar tried all the downstairs windows, until he found one he could prize open with a penknife, helped the lady into a small window of what proved to be the gentlemen's cloakroom, and vanished silently into the night unseen by hotel staff or any of his parishioners.

But as the slow intermittent trek home started . . a trek to be sharply reversed when the bombing of Manchester actually started in 1940 . . it was found that many children had learnt to appreciate the pleasures of the country, as had quite a few of the mothers and many had formed ties which were to be maintained. A few - very few - boys remained to work on the land, and girls to help with domestic or dairy work on the farms, or to go 'into service'.

This brings to mind another picture, more gilded perhaps than all those others by the golden September sunshine which so blessedly shone on the labours of those first few months, of children transformed in a very short time by a new mode of living, for marvellous changes were wrought in many by improved physical health. In some cases a few short weeks seem to have brought about that development of personality which teachers and educators seek to achieve through an educational scheme covering many years.

One of the brightest memories was of sixteen girls from a school in one of the most poverty-stricken areas of Manchester. They were billeted together in the village inn, cared for by the inn-keeper's wife, a woman of stout commonsense and great kindness of heart.

A room was set apart for the girls' dining-room, a large pleasant room with red-tiled floor, and two long tables covered with white American cloth. They had good meals, porridge with unlimited milk, eggs and bread-and-butter for breakfast, an excellent two-course dinner, with fresh vegetables and wholesome puddings, a good 'high tea', and early to bed. A large room at the top of the inn was converted into a comfortable dormitory. "Lights Out" sounded early, but their foster-mother always went up to have a chat with each girl and see them settled for the night.

During the sunny weather the girls did their own washing in the clean cobbled inn-yard. 'Grandad' sat on his chair in the sun, and the girls were taught that they must always be kind and courteous to him. Sometimes he turned the handle of the big wooden mangle for them, and gave them apples and sweets.

The girls sat in the sun with him, and read and knitted. They went for country walks, to Church or Sunday School, and on Saturday were conducted into the market town to spend their pocket-money.

Everything was clean and bright as a new pin, and so the girls looked too, and their new-found vivacity and friendliness suggested that they had found something fresh and worthwhile in life.

Many people still living in the areas concerned may well remember those searing days . . . the motherly ones who wept over the deprived scraps of humanity sent into their care;   the gentle ones intimidated by the young toughs of both sexes bred in the squalor of the slums . . . and there *were* slums in Manchester in those days . . . and the efficient ones nearly driven to breaking-point by sluttish mothers, the cause of whose shortcomings they could never begin to understand.

But the qualities that stand out most in my memory were the unfailing kindness and sympathy of the hosts, both in homes and schools, under the most trying conditions.

I remember too the hard work and utter dedication of the teachers who were themselves torn from their homes and family responsibilities in such grave times, and those native ones who had to put up with the alien invasion.   All were working in an unfamiliar situation, with no precedent or example to follow, and no code of regulations but that of sympathy and common sense to guide them.

I often wondered how many of these youngsters remained permanently to become integrated into Shropshire life, and could now give their own impressions . . a child's memories . . of that great upheaval.

CHAPTER XI

MY AUNTS & GRANDMOTHERS

My two Grandmothers and my aunts were of consider-
able importance in our young lives. Of the former, both
lived in Sheffield, and when we visited we always stayed at the
'stern' paternal granny's and made teatime excursions to the
'jolly' one. They lived on opposite sides of the city, and to
go from one suburb to the other by tram-car would have been
a long and arduous trip. But there was a shorter cross-country
route which took us through a strange little lane called Frog
Walk. This was on a steep hill, a flagged path bordered on
both sides by high stone walls, with dense woodland on one
side, and a rushing torrent on the other. To me, this 'shut'
or 'ginnel' was spooky and frightening even in bright daylight;
and I was thankful when we emerged onto a broad tree-lined
road which led to the quiet close where tucked away was
granny's interesting split-level house.

My maternal granny . . . so different from my mother . . .
was jolly, lovable and amusing. Indeed, she was so comical
that my brother and I would be helpless with laughter at her
mimicries; and we always felt that she was, as are so many
grannies, 'on our side'. On one occasion, when my mother
was anxiously rounding us up to return to 'stern' grandmother's, I heard granny say, "Don't be so *severe* with them,
Lucy; they're not doing any harm; they're only enjoying
themselves!"

Another little grandson, our cousin, was deeply devoted.
I remember seeing him sitting in her ample lap, and tears
welled into his bright brown eyes as he leaned against her
ample bosom, and her arms folded round him. She was highly
corseted and boned, and I recollect my young brother asking
why "she had such a high shelf on her chest". This amused
her enormously, but embarrassed my mother, who hushed him
up with pursed lips.

This granny sang operatic arias, read Byron at the breakfast table, and loved going to the theatre. An aunt told me
later how my mother, a young girl at home, was taken to
matinees, which were usually light comedies and very popular
with leisured ladies. As soon as they settled in the hot theatre

my mother started swaying about, whispered that she was 'feeling faint' and must go out; at which my grandmother gave her a push and told her briskly "to be quiet and sit up; they were *both* there to enjoy the play", whereupon my mother sat up and remained composed throughout.

This dear granny died at only sixty-four, owing, we heard the rumour, to an impulsive and ill-advised second marriage, to a rich Swede who proved to be rather a villain.

My stern paternal grandmother couldn't have been more different. She died before the 1914 war at the age of ninety-four. She had been the Headmistress or Lady Superintendent of a Seminary for Young Ladies at Newbury in Berkshire; and I think of her pupils as characters in a Jane Austen novel.

I can see her now, sitting in her rocking-chair between the piano and the chenille-covered table, on which lay her Bible and the daily paper, together with the wire-rimmed spectacles needed to decipher their small print. Her voluminous black satin skirt just disclosed the polished toes of her laced-up boots, her boned bodice was heavy with black jet and lace trimming, with a white ruff at the neck.

From the age of forty-two, when she was considered to be 'getting on', she had her breakfast taken up to bed. I remember one occasion when we young children, chatting in the hall below, happened to mention the word 'dancing'. Grandmother, majestically descending the stairs at mid-day, was heard to mutter, "Dancing! Dancing! Such levity, an invention of the devil - let me hear no more of it!" Looking back, I find her remark rather strange, as surely her young ladies would have had lessons from a dancing-master?

My last memory of her was seeing her in her bedroom, where each wall was a trellis of roses so vivid and natural that I used to fancy that I could smell their scent. There she lay in her big double bed with the white honeycomb counterpane, her small hands, heavy with rings, laid neatly on the soft delaine sheet, the centre parting of her crisp silvery hair changed from rosy pink to marble white.

Some old toys had been kept at 'stern' granny's for our indoor entertainment; a solitaire board complete with marbles, a Halma board with its 'little men'; and a huge box of plain wooden building blocks which included arches and pillars, and other fancy pieces. A packet of Snap cards completed the collection. And then there were books, of course, early editions of "Alice" and "Fauntleroy", "The Water Babies" and "Peter Pan", and of course the beloved "Little Women". "Grimm's Fairy Tales" looked as grim as its name, with its dark brown cover and gloomy illustrations, but we treasured it greatly. Two bound volumes of "Little

Folks" reduced my brother to derisive laughter. Most of the stories seemed to involve ill-used young chimney-sweeps, but there were plenty about namby-pamby little girls in upperclass households who usually expired from low fever or bad consciences. There were also horrid schoolgirls jealous of each other's pretty frocks, or stealing sweetmeats, which crimes received their due reward, or were repented of and forgiven.

It was different at 'jolly' granny's; no toys as such had been preserved, but there were other delights. A treadle sewing-machine, for one. Granny would give us scraps of material and we would sit in turn furiously working the foot-treadle, and fiddling with the gadgets in the tool-box. Best of all was a pianola or mechanical piano, which had been a present to Granny from the gentleman who became her second husband. The foot-pedal was worked in similar fashion to the sewing-machine, and by inserting spiked brass cylinders inside the instrument the most wonderful music could be produced . . . Tosti's "Goodbye", "The Lost Chord", and airs from the operas, and no one seemed to mind how long we sat working away and producing incredible volumes of sound.

The pleasures offered by the garden were simple but adequate for our one-day trips. There was a stout wooden cart in which we pushed each other down the steep drive which led from front to back garden. Then we chased each other round the split-level house, running down into the cellar, and emerging from a door at garden level.

One of our aunts, daughter of 'stern' granny, and sister to my father, became an Inspector of Schools. She was, in fact, one of the first four women inspectors ever to be appointed, called from a college lecture-ship to the staff of one Hon. Maud Lawrence, Head of the newly-appointed Female Inspectorate of the London Education Authority.

She was a small lady, this aunt, exquisitely dressed, with mounds of silvery hair, and a blue eye so keen that a single glint from her convex rimless lenses was enough to make a tall headmaster cringe before her. She had a spacious flat in Kensington, and was a member of the "Ladies' Alpine Club" in Bond Street. We had photographs of her about to attack the Matterhorn or some such peak, attired in an ankle-length tweed skirt and a large hat, and surrounded by sundry coiled ropes, alpenstocks and ice-axes.

When she came to stay with us we had to stand to attention while she inspected our hair, ears, teeth, and finger-nails; commented on our clothes, and assessed our reading ability in English and in French. My mother, who should have addressed some rather brisk words to her, fluttered nervously by during this examination.

But the aunt was also very kind, and used to send me exotic presents from Switzerland and Italy, toys when young, and jewels and scarves in my adolescence. Moreover, during the latter period, I was dressed almost exclusively in her cast-offs, tailored costumes and silk blouses which fitted me perfectly; and large velour hats which had to be sent to the cleaners to be reblocked into suitable shapes.

One early Christmas I received from her a beautiful green velvet dress, *new*, from Liberty's. The trouble was it had little silk frills on the shoulders instead of proper sleeves; and I, of course, was wearing woollen combinations with sleeves to the elbows. As party-time approached, I begged my mother to be allowed to wear different underwear. But, no. I stood impatiently while she pushed up the thick woollen sleeves into my armpits and tacked them into tight rolls on my shoulders. During the party these woolly lumps with their large white tacking-stitches continually descended from under the green frills, and I spent the whole party-time anxiously pushing them up out of sight of the derisive eyes of my little friends. To add to this shaming situation I had a large white baby shawl wrapped and pinned round over my best coat, 'because I had only a thin frock underneath.'

At thirteen years of age puberty descended upon me, details of its manifestations having been disclosed to me in lowered tones between the coats in the games cloakroom. From my mother no information was forthcoming, and she obviously regarded the subject as unmentionable until it was forced upon her attention.

And so, one fine Saturday morning, finding me engaged in happy, healthy outdoor activity, she drew me in from the garden, conducted me solemnly upstairs, and put me to bed. Seated on the end of it, and gazing at me with an expression of acute anxiety, not to say anguish, she proceeded to outline the future course of my life.

Henceforward, "at certain times, I must not" she said, "bathe, swim, paddle, wash my hair, eat prunes or other opening foods, stand barefoot on cold surfaces, wash my hands in cold water, stand on my feet too long, or ride a bicycle! Moreover I must now wear longer skirts, and cease to play cricket and football or climb trees with my brother and his friends." "And", she concluded, "if you do not obey me in all these things, you will have *dreadful diseases* in middle age!" I lay back feeling ill already, and decided that life as I knew it, was finished.

However, some months later a small incident considerably changed my outlook for the better. In the chemistry lab one day I asked a friend to wash out a test-tube for me.

"Right-o", she said, "but why can't you do it yourself?"

"I -er - mustn't put my hands in cold water."

"Oh, why not; got a rash or something?"

"Well - er ---" In all seriousness, I recited my mother's long list of proscribed activities. "You see, ' "The Curse is come upon me!" cried the Lady of Shallott," ' I added, muttering the current euphemism. She stared at me with popping eyes. "Go on! *Do* tell us what else you can't do!" "Couldn't you warm them over your bunsen burner afterwards?" A small crowd gathered round my bench. Hoots of laughter brought the science mistress into our midst.

Suddenly it flashed upon me that there might be other opinions in the world more valid than my mother's. Was it possible that she might be wrong? that her ideas were not universal? Then possibly all her other dire admonishments and forebodings were not shared by the rest of the world, were just peculiar ideas of her own?

I felt as if a ray of sunshine had burst upon me, as though a fresh breeze were blowing away a lot of dark clouds.

Remembering the anxiety and gloom that seemed to surround every innocent and trivial incident, I henceforward examined all of her edicts and utterances, and subjected them to the light of reason and common sense, and, above all, to the touchstone of general opinion.

The episode of the green dress puts me in mind of a much more grave disappointment connected with a much-loved sister of my mother's. A sister, yes, but oh, so different! This aunt, a language mistress at a girls' high school was so jolly, so carefree and adventurous, and understanding. The only thing that bothered us about her was that, taking us for walks, she *would* wear a knee-length hockey skirt, bright blue, with a broad band of yellow braid round its twirling hem. Since skirts were then ankle-length, this exhibition deeply embarrassed my brother, who one day dared to tell her he didn't like to be seen with it. He got such a crisp answer that we realised that we couldn't take liberties even with this aunt.

Anyway, she got engaged to a dashing young captain in the first World War. How glamorous he looked in his khaki uniform with cavalry trousers and a soft peaked cap! Somehow it came to my ears that she wanted me to be a 'child Bridesmaid' at her wedding, but, of course I was not told openly until a decision had been made. Need I say the answer was 'no' . . . "the expense of the dress," "the trouble" . . . "a girl is best sitting quietly with her mother". . . . . But I think a fear of emotion of any kind, a dislike of ceremony,

was behind her decision.   I had to sit in the pew and watch
the horrid little fat girl from next door standing behind my
aunt, carrying her bouquet and wearing a gorgeous cream
lace dress with a flounced skirt.

Other deprivations followed.   A dancing-mistress
attended our little dame establishment once a week to give
lessons after school.   As I prepared to go straight home, I
watched with tearful envy my friends changing into their
frilly dresses and bronze dancing-pumps.   But. . . 'dancing-
lessons are not really necessary' and 'it is best to come
straight home to tea at the proper time.'

The Girl Guides?   How I longed to join!   But no, 'it
was not safe to go out in the evenings', and 'didn't know
what class of girl I might meet', 'would get my death of cold
in those dreadful muddy camps.'

More acute disappointments followed, one at least
owing wholly to my mother's tender care of me, and also
connected with an aunt;   the other having a much more
prolonged influence on my life.   This other aunt of mine
married a captain in the French army, the 'Paris aunt' we
called her.   Their rare visits to us were occasions of great
excitement.   He examined our spoken French, gave us
French coins, and told us many tales of his travels and army
experiences.   Alas, this uncle was killed outright by a bomb
which fell into the midst of a group of officers 'somewhere
in France'.   My widowed aunt, who was clever, musical,
sociable and ambitious, and a member of the "Acadamie
Francaise", lost no time in setting herself up in a luxury
apartment in Paris, where she built up a connection as tutor
in English to the children of the French aristocracy;   and in
this capacity she travelled the world as a sort of superior
governess to the offspring of counts and dukes.

When I was a little over fifteen years old, a faint rumour
reached my ears that this aunt had invited me to spend a year
with her to 'finish', and perfect my French;   and this to
include travelling with her on any of her 'educational
journeys'.   I dare not let my mind dwell on this heady
prospect, as I knew only too well what the reply might be.
Not only was the offer declined, but I remember well the
tone of voice in which my mother expressed her opinion of
it.   "As if I *would* let you go!   No knowing *what* might
happen!   Imagine her suggesting such a thing!"   The sense of
guilt. . . *my* guilt for even wanting to go, oppressed me for a
long time.   My father did not even take me or my mother to
Paris for the funeral of the aunt, which occurred some two
years later.   I gathered from scraps of conversation that it
was an extraordinary 'affair, with many notable people

present, and her 'salon' literally lined with flowers from floor to ceiling. Even to attend that would have been something! One memorial of her life and death I have with me still. . . a set of rose-pink pure silk damask curtains from that same salon, from which I had constructed an elaborate evening coat, still hanging in my wardrobe draped in a plastic bag.

As time went on there was markedly less resistance to my brother's claim to freedom; though he was still somewhat subject to my father's harsh discipline, and I well remember an incident which illustrates this. My brother, an undergraduate at Manchester University, was to take me to the annual students' ball. Father, rather surprisingly, offered him a house key, to avoid his being disturbed on our return; and with strict instructions to be home by half past ten.

We had a good time at the ball; my dance programme was full, and we had a lovely supper of sausage rolls, trifle and lemonade. Tearing ourselves regretfully away we managed to be in the porch soon after ten-thirty, only to realise that my brother had forgotten to pick up the key. I watched him turn pale with fear as my father appeared at the door in his dressing-gown, angrily demanding what we thought we were up to, being so careless and irresponsible.

I remember one bit of defiance on my own part which seemed to pay off without terrible retribution at home, though with unfortunate results at school. My Latin mistress, who was also my form mistress, summoned me to her desk after prayers one morning. Her face was white, and her voice trembled with what I took to be fury.

"What happened to you last night? Where did you go? I want a full explanation!"

What had happened last night was that Form IV Alpha had been taken by her and the senior English mistress to see the Sir Frank Benson Company in a Shakespeare play at the Manchester Opera House. We were taken by special coach, and were told to assemble in the foyer after the play to receive instructions about the journey home. Three of us had secretly taken autograph books, and in the jostle to get out had escaped by a side entrance and rushed to the stage door to try to see Sir Frank. The great man kept us waiting a very, very long time, but we managed to waylay him and were rewarded with his signature in each of our books under the quotation "Our true intent is all for your delight".

Gleefully we ran round to the front of the theatre to find that the coach, the school party, and everyone else had departed, and the great doors were being closed. Nothing daunted we walked to the centre of the City and found the right tram-cars to take us to our respective homes. None of us gave a thought to the coach kept waiting in the hopes of our turning up, nor to the anxiety of the responsible mistresses. To my surprise, my mother seemed to assume without question that we had been properly escorted home, and all she said was, "You're very late; you must go straight to bed". But what a terrible night Miss L. must have had wondering where we had got to and thinking about what awful fate might have befallen us!

It was this same Latin mistress who was associated with one of my keenest disappointments, brought about by my mother wholly in the best interests of my welfare. But that is a story that will keep; because its effects are with me still, in the form of fading resentment, and the faint scars of a chip on the shoulder.

CHAPTER XII

AWAY FROM HOME

It was the year 1925 and I was now about twenty years old and embarked on an entirely new mode of life. The rooms recommended to me by the grocer's shop were in a terraced Edwardian house in a quiet cul-de-sac. I was offered the front sitting-room with bay, the best bedroom above it, and use of bathroom. My landlady was also to light coal fires as necessary, and to do my washing. For this accommodation and services she asked fifteen shillings a week, but I paid her an extra five and sixpence to cook me an evening meal six nights a week and lunch on Sunday.

Her husband was a jobbing gardener, a lanky, slow-moving fellow, with indifferent health and a meagre and intermittent wage. This was supplemented by nice little sums of prize money from his absorbing hobby. This was the rearing of Chinese bantam cockerels. Before each Show these birds were brought in one at a time, and placed on newspaper on the kitchen table. He then dressed their multi-coloured plumage with a special oil which made them look like creatures of brilliant enamel. Afterwards he gave each bird a lump of sugar dipped in whiskey because that 'moide thoy vurry frisky'. Their prize rosettes adorned the walls of their living-room.

My landlady, Mrs. Axton, had perforce another source of income, which was the taking in of laundry-work. She seemed to specialise in 'whites' which she did for a number of the big county houses. Behind the kitchen was a scullery with a huge built-in brick boiler. It had an iron-doored furnace beneath, and a copper-lined vat. She lit the fire first thing in the morning, then washed her assorted pile of linen in a zinc tub with a rubbing-board. All was then man-handled into the foaming vat for half an hour's boiling. How she got it all dry was a miracle, but more miraculous was the final ironing.

For this she used flat, or 'sad' irons heated on the coal range, and an old blanket and sheet, on the rough wooden table. Huge double-damask table-cloths were screen-folded and rolled into what looked like segments of marble pillar.

Like bas-relief carving, too, were the heavily-embroidered afternoon tea-cloths. But she specialised in gentlemen's evening dress, stiff white shirts and wing-colours. These had to be rubbed through a special starch, and finally polished with a curved polishing-iron, also heated on live coals. When finished they looked as if moulded of white porcelain. The mountain of completed work had the pure whiteness, with blue shadows, of Alpine snow. Not a mark, not a coal smut or speck of dust from the bathbrick cleaning-board, sullied the finished articles.

When wrapped and strung up in brown paper, these bundles were carried out by her husband, trudging along the country roads; or sometimes a chauffeur in a motor-car called for the more opulent loads; and she charged an average of two shillings and sixpence for each wash.

I did not teach in a school, but in a long, low building which was the old cottage hospital admirably converted into a Training Centre where the senior girls from all the schools in the town came for instruction in the domestic arts and sciences. There were but two of us on the staff, my senior, an elderly widow, and myself. A bright young red-head worked in a separate sort of out-house which I understood to have been the old mortuary. There she taught, happily and successfully, a group of so-called 'Mental Defectives'.

There seemed to be little social or cultural life in the town; and everyone seemed to me very old or very young. I went to church, and later joined a small play-reading group. Apart from this every night I spent in my quiet room, working hard preparing lessons, or, for recreation reading, doing dressmaking and embroidery; the only sounds to be heard being the thud of Mrs. Axten's iron or the occasional squawk of her husband's frisky birds.

Despite my earnest attempts to leave home, I had to admit that I was feeling rather lonely. I missed my brother and all our friends; the former, now living an independent life of his own, was seldom at home at the time of my visits there.

Time and time again I asked myself if it was my fault that these visits seemed more of a duty than a pleasure. We never enjoyed a happy and carefree exchange of news; and I was conscious that my parents were always assessing me . . . my physical health, my clothes, appearance, behaviour. This was especially so at table when their watchfulness made me feel unable to eat. This exacerbated the situation, increasing my mother's anxious scrutiny, and my own nervous unease. Anorexia nervosa was a malady unheard of then.

Back in my rooms, my circumscribed life began to widen a little. My landlady took another lodger, a young lad called Reg who 'lived with the family'. He was a trainee clerk on the railways, and used to cycle down each day on a push-bike. I was encouraged to buy a second-hand bike; and although it had missing spokes and an old oil-lamp tied on with string, I pedalled many miles with him over the country side. We visited Henley Regatta, toured stately homes, and picnicked in the woods and fields. He soon left, but I continued these expeditions alone, and with books and sandwiches in my saddlebag explored the beauties of the Thames Valley. Sometimes I went on a "Go-Anywhere" cheap day bus trip; and I remember on one outing through the entrancing autumn woodlands of the Chiltern Hills hearing an old gentleman say, "Ah, if earth is so beautiful, what can heaven be?"

Then social life expanded a little more. Two friends of my brother's happened to obtain posts respectively in and near London, and both contacted me, thinking I might be lonely, and regarding us all somewhat as exiles from home. As a result I used to take a Saturday train up to London, and was either taken to the moving pictures or for a ride on an open-top bus, with tea afterwards at a Lyon's Corner House.

Or one or other of them would call for me at my rooms, and we would go for long hikes in the lovely footpaths and woodlands of Buckinghamshire. We were all fond of poetry and would sometimes sit in a London park or some woodland glade reading favourite poems to each other.

A snap of me, taken by the companion of one such outing, shows me wearing a long-skirted tweed costume, tailored by myself, a broad-brimmed felt hat, whose crown was distorted into a curious oval shape by the large plaited coils of hair over each ear. This style was considered more youthful and attractive than the spinsterish bun at the back. In my case these 'earphones' were of such enormous size that it took twelve hairpins a side to attach them to my scalp. Since this rendered all hats very tight the pins stuck most painfully into my ears and temples. If I wriggled a finger up to relieve the pressure, an ungainly hank of hair would descend, dangling hairpins down my cheek. A rucksack on my back, laced-up boots, leather gloves, and a stout walking-stick completed my ensemble.

Any outfit less conducive to sentimentality or flirtatiousness, or 'hanky-panky' of any kind it would be hard to imagine. But then, the boys we knew would not dream of taking liberties, and the code of our 'set' outlawed such behaviour as "soppy". I am reminded of an incident at one of the dances at the "University House". A whisper went round that two people had been seen kissing and embracing on the landing outside the drawing-room. . . that beautiful Aladdin's cave of a room where we floated around in candle-light and incense-vapour. . . They proved to be an officially engaged young couple, but their conduct was considered rather daring and really 'not quite nice'. If my mother had known of such goings-on she would not have let me attend such a den of vice.

Another small social episode comes to mind which threw a different light on things. One of my brother's university friends was a fair attractive Dane, the lucky owner of a dashing red sports car. This gave him added glamour since none of us aspired any higher than an old push-bike. Several of us were chatting idly at home trying to decide whether to go and play tennis, and I happened to say, "Well, I must just run out to the post-box first with a letter." At once the Dane offered to take me in his gorgeous car. "Thanks very much, I said, but it really isn't worth it; the post-box is only at the end of our road." A girl standing near said to me later, "Why *on earth* did you refuse his offer? You should have accepted, directed him to a post-box miles and miles away, admired his car, thanked him for a lovely trip. . . and of course he would have asked you again. . . . and again. . . You really don't know how to manage things, do you?" she finished scornfully. Her words quite opened my eyes, and I wondered if some important side of my education had been sadly neglected.

Meanwhile, in my letters home I related in detail all my activities, though I had no need to do so since no member of the family ever visited me in my rooms. My mother's letters gave a little mild news, followed by admonishments about woollen vests, good food and early nights. What a surprise it was therefore, to receive from her a letter, backed up by one from my father, reminding me severely that I was approaching twenty-one, must take life seriously, and watch my step. The gist of the letter was that I must cease forthwith from meeting these friends of my youth, as "it was bad for my reputation to be seen having young men call for me at my lodgings." It never occurred to me to do other than obey, though I grieved for years after, not only for happy times lost, but because I felt quite unable to explain to these sensible and good-hearted young men, whom I had known from about nine years old, why I had so suddenly terminated our pleasant meetings.

I had now begun to use a little make-up, if such it could be called; some wet, bubbly vanishing-cream which spurted from a small tube costing sixpence-halfpenny, and some vaseline to shine up the lids and lips in a most sensuous manner. I also smoked the occasional cigarette. . . Egyptian or Russian, in a nine-inch ivory holder. These fast habits, however, I discarded on my visits home. How nostalgic are these small personal bygones! The swansdown puffs with pleated satin backs and ivory handles, the hair-combs with diamante borders, the dance-programmes with their tiny pink or white pencils, the fans, so pretty and varied, the long dangling ear-rings, the ivory or ebony cigarette-holder, the artificial flower corsages. . . One slung one's fan and programme from the left wrist where it bobbed against one's partner's back, while he delicately held one's left shoulder with a white-gloved hand.

But dancing was not for me in those early days of my career. If my mother had known it, she might have had some genuine small worry about my health, which had begun to decline from its usual robust state. I was interested to note that my symptoms were similar to those of my landlady's husband, namely, spots, feeble appetite, lethargy and depression. I began to give some thought to her cooking methods, which were designed to give maximum time to the all-important laundrywork. When she rose at six in the morning she lighted both fires, the coal range and the little furnace under the copper. She then prepared and cooked all the food required for the whole day. This was set out on plates and reheated in the fire-oven as needed, even up to midnight.

I had a meagre breakfast because I couldn't afford a cooked one, and a snack lunch. My evening meal came to me on a blazing hot plate; some curls of brown meat with black edges, dried-up vegetables all set in a sizzling rim of gummy gravy. A slice of stodgy pudding received the same treatment; and if there was a sauce one could lift its surface like a hard lid revealing a yellow sticky mass beneath.

Now vitamins were practically unknown at that time to the general public. It was in 1912 that Sir Frederick Gowland Hopkins discovered, through experiments with rats, that there was a factor, vital to good health, found only in fresh foods. This was allied to the proteins, and therefore to the amino-acids, so was called an amine, and, by its nature, a vita-amine. Even the large tome on food science, our standard college book of reference, made little mention of the subject; and it was years before the whole range of vitamins, from A and D, and C through the important B-complex, and E and K, were isolated and their functions understood.

With hindsight I realise that freshly-cooked vegetables and meat, or a multi-vitamin pill, if such had been known, would have rapidly corrected our troubles. Meanwhile Mrs. A. continued to dress her husband's boils, and I treated mine to a waft of crude pink powder for rare social occasions.

The latter began to increase, and for a year or two I enjoyed my work, small town life, and the beauties of the countryside. In winter there was the added pleasure of celebrity concerts at a nearby girls boarding-school, to which the Principal very courteously invited all local teachers as guests. Here I heard the famous Goossens family, Cortot, the violinist Jelli D'Aranyi, and the cellist Beatrice Harrison who had had recordings made of herself playing in the woods to inspire the nightingales, and achieving wonderful duets with them.

But now my parents' health began to decline a little, and I felt it was time to go back north. I obtained a new post with a better salary, and arranged to live at home again, but determined to have an independent life and enter into all the activities which had been so restricted in my girlhood.

Accordingly I attended classes in English literature, languages, singing and music, journalism, Greek dancing . . . I also went to theatres and concerts, travelled abroad, and went on adventurous cruises alone. There were no package holidays in those days.

I remember the world-famous soprano Galli Curci making a final "Final Appearance" at the Free Trade Hall in Manchester. The audience was embarrassed by her creaking notes; she cracked completely with an agonised grimace on top C, curtsied briefly, swiftly left the stage; and never appeared in public again. I remember being present at the first public performance of Yehudi Menuhin, a little lad of eleven or twelve in a velvet knickerbocker suit.

It was usual for good plays with top players to open in Manchester before being transferred to the West End stage, because the 'north' was considered a more critical audience. I saw there many famous actors and actresses at the beginning of their careers. . . . Olivier, Guilgud, Wolfit, Marie Lohr, Athene Seyler, Henry Ainley, Sir Frank Benson, Alan Badel, Ralph Richardson and Gwen Francon-Davis in the splendid "Richard of Bordeaux" by the woman playwright Gordon Daviot; the famous Lunts, and many others.

Comic actors in those days were 'gentlemen' . . . little Leslie Henson at his piano, the corpulent Fred Emney with his monacle; Seymour Hicks, a charming man whose by-play with his tie had the audience rocking in their seats. Then there was Sonnie Hale and his sister Binnie, all deliciously funny without being vulgar.

As for ballet, there was the legendary Pavlova in her prime. She was bony and brittle with a sharp, wan face, but when she danced the "Dragonfly" irrediscent, fluttering, darting, you would swear that not a toe, not a wing-tip touched the ground. And her "Dying Swan". . . floating, not on ground apparently, but on water, calm and serene, her beautiful curving neck held aloft, then sinking, her wings slowly closing over her in death. . . what magic, what genius! I also saw her dancing the lead in "Giselle", "Swan Lake", and "Les Sylphides"; and it was of one of these performances that a reviewer spoke of the 'sad and mysterious poetry of her performance'.

I recall the first night of Sybil Thorndike in Shaw's "Saint Joan", and coming out from the Opera House in pouring rain. It was the custom in those days to wear full evening dress with jewels to concert and theatre, even without male escort. But my dreadful old second-hand car broke down, and two of us girls in long floating dresses and velvet cloaks pushed it into a muddy gutter, and stood waiting in our fancy silver shoes for some kind man to come along and help us, which they usually did.

But now the 1914/18 war was long forgotten, as was the General Strike of 1926, when complete disruption of services and industrial life was averted by the extraordinary spirit of patriotism and mutual helpfulness which prevailed. Students and business men alike took enthusiastically to jobs quite alien to them, and the young worked in a spirit of huge fun and adventure. I remember being driven to work each day by a youngster in a horse-drawn Irish jaunting-car. The Great Jarrow Hunger March, and the unemployment and Depression of the Thirties were things of the past.

The general stability and peacefulness of society was well illustrated by the country's reaction to an unprecedented event . . the murder of a police constable by a villain called Charlie Peace. Waves of horror and consternation reverberated round the land for weeks. The policeman was buried in a country churchyard close to where we lived, and on his headstone was carved a replica of the Force's helmet. For long after, people came, not so much in pilgrimage as in curiosity, to see the grave of the killer's victim. The headstone was finally removed to the Police Museum.

People generally could safely leave their houses unlocked; young girls could walk home late at night or alone in woodland or country lane without fear of molestation.

But in Germany, Hitler was rising to power. I remember being there early in 1938, and being struck by the monster banners slung across new buildings, bridges, and housing developments bearing the Nazi emblem of the crooked cross, and proclaiming fulsome praise to the Fuhrer for his "great works for the Fatherland". Even the normal greetings of 'guten Tag' or 'gute Nacht' were replaced by "Heil Hitler!" and the Nazi salute. Once, on entering public lavatories we were given this rather impersonal welcome by attendants guarding the doors. My companion responded with the Navy salute and a brisk "God save the King!", which satirical gesture earned us a suspicious and hostile stare.

But we did not take Hitler very seriously then, and were almost as unprepared to defend ourselves as in the 1914 war; and rumbles of the next conflict were still afar off.

73

CHAPTER XIII

REMEMBRANCE OF THINGS PAST

When I returned home, about 1927, I obtained a new and more remunerative post, and lived a life of greater freedom. Among the many interests already described was the membership of a society started in Cheshire by two Quaker Brothers who were interested in both drama and mountain-climbing.

In winter we produced amateur plays and concerts; and in summer, starting at Easter, spent camping weekends in Derbyshire and longer holidays in the Lake District. Lakeland was not then a tourist centre for 'trippers', and most visitors were bona fide fell-walkers. There were no cafes, kiosks, or souvenir shops; no coach parties, or pleasure steamers on the lakes. Apart from the few big hotels, there were modest bed-and-breakfast places, and rather primitive cottages and farms. Sometimes a group of us rented the latter, but mostly we camped, travelling up there in ramshackle cars, and sleeping in make-shift tents. When fine, we slept under the stars, cooked and ate out-of-doors, and sang folk-songs round a camp-fire in the evenings. On Sundays we often went to Early Communion before starting the day's climb, and I remember seeing the small church porch crammed with rucksacks and climbing gear, while nailed boots clattered up the aisle.

In time we 'bagged' all the peaks. In March and April the weather was unpredictable, and I recall finding ourselves on the summit of Scafell Pike in a heavy snow-storm and swirling mist. Rigid with cold and hunger, our hands too cold to open lunch packs, we huddled round the cairn feeling we could perish on the spot. But one of the company was a good mountaineer, and with a compass and much encouragement, he got us down to safety.

I often wondered if my mother worried much about these expeditions, but if so she did not show so much anxiety, and seldom asked many questions about our activities.

Some time after I married and left home for good, my father became an invalid, but neither of them gave the slightest consideration to the idea of his going to hospital. For over three years my mother gradually tired herself out nursing him with uncomplaining devotion. My poor father, so very severe, yet so anxious for our welfare . . . after he had finally to go to hospital became pathetic and child-like; his only words, repeated endlessly, and incapable of being granted, were "Take me home . . . I want to go home!"

After his death my mother rapidly regained her health. Her complexion had the bloom of youth, and there was scarcely a grey hair in her head. We helped her to turn her house into two flats, and she let the upper one to a pleasant young woman, the Principal of a Teacher Training College. This arrangement worked very well, and she tried to re-establish a modest social life.

One weekend, when her tenant happened to be away, we had planned a small tea-party for her to meet some old friends. I telephoned to see if she was ready to be fetched, but there was no reply. Perhaps she was in the garden? in the bath? upstairs? I made call after call, and heard the phone ringing in a silent house. Filled with foreboding we rushed over, and peering through a leaded coloured glass window had a distorted vision of her, apparently lifeless, lying at the foot of the stairs.

The police had to be fetched to break into the locked house, and she was taken away in an ambulance. Police. . . ambulance. . . hospital. . . how she would have loathed and dreaded to be associated with such affairs! But she had had a massive stroke, no doubt the result of the strain of two World Wars, and the long nursing of my father.

I visited her twice a day, to watch over her, and help feed her, but she was without speech and helpless, and never knew me. And then, at the end of about a fortnight, one afternoon, there suddenly came into her unseeing eyes a sharp gleam of recognition. She uttered, not my name, but that of my young daughter; and then, quite clearly and distinctly asked 'if someone would play a hymn for her'. There being no possible means of producing such music, I sang, oblivious of others, a verse of "Abide with Me", it being the first thing that came into my head. As I sang, she kept her eyes on me, but gradually they closed, and there came over her face that change that is like no other change. "Abide with Me" is a tear-jerking tune at the best of times, but I can never hear it now without feeling a deep but time-worn emotion.

Now my memory stretches back to the friends of my youth. Where are they now? The Lakeland circle is long scattered and departed. Of my women friends of long standing, only three remain; and of those who were at the same school as myself, it is interesting to note that all did well in life, many in important if not prestigious posts, which was a tribute to our rather stern education.

Of my brother's friends, the beautiful Dane with the scarlet car returned to his native land and was seen no more. A geography student friend became a mountaineer and perished in a climbing accident. Of the two with whom I fraternised in London and in the country, one inherited a fortune from his father but renounced the bequest and bought a cottage in the Lakes, wandered solitary on the fells, wrote poetry, published some books, and finally died young and rather mysteriously in his remote home. The other went out to India, became a colonel in the British Army of the Raj, and married the daughter of an Indian Civil Servant. Now he is a sad widower, living alone, a frail and aged man, but caring for a mentally-afflicted son, victim of a childhood meningitis wrongly diagnosed and treated in an Indian hospital.

And my brother, the companion and playmate of my childhood? He also lived a sad life as a widower, retired to a small home on the coast of Anglesey. He played the piano, the clarinet and the banjo, had an occasional game of golf, a weekly pub meeting with a friend, and lavished affection on a little dog. He was a tall strong man with thick wavy hair, and a weather-brown face; and he looked remarkably youthful for his age.

But, while he was out walking alone with his dog on an empty beach, he, like my mother, most unexpectedly suffered a severe stroke. We were told that his dog, barking furiously and leaping round him as he lay in the sand, led to his discovery some hours later. He was taken to the local hospital, thence to the main one at Bangor; and finally to a terminal ward in a huddle of grey huts in the centre of Anglesey.

On my last visit, driving through the mountains towards the sea, I felt that, as in Hardy's novels, the weather matched the mood of the times. The black, forbidding peaks, swathed in mist, were reflected in the inky depths of the lakes; but over the Straits, drifting rain cast a wet, grey blanket over the featureless landscape.

I arrived in time; the doctor gave my brother about twenty minutes to live. He was breathing heavily and deeply unconscious; but I was determined to get through to some non-perished part of his brain. I spoke some words of comfort, and repeated them over and over and over again like a record whose needle has stuck in a groove. This may have sounded foolish to those standing by, but it worked like a miracle. His hand came to life and slowly pressed mine. His taut, distressed features relaxed, and softened into the sweetest and most heavenly smile I have ever seen on a human face. A moment later, he breathed a long sigh, and passed into some realm distant from our own. Briefly, I felt a curious kind of envy; and then, if I had not believed it beore, I believed at that moment, that there is some other world beyond our present one.

On my return journey, passing through the small town where he had lived, I noticed that the sun, perversely, was shining brilliantly, but I felt that it, and my childhood, had been blotted out for ever. Sentimental as they may sound, Masefield's words express my thoughts:

"I think of the friends who are dead, who were dear
long ago in the past,
Beautiful friends who are dead, though I know that
death cannot last;
Friends with the beautiful eyes that the dust has defiled;
Beautiful souls who were gentle when I was a child."

Or Charles Lamb's

"So might we talk of the old familiar faces. . .
How some they have died, and some they have left me,
And some are taken from me; all are departed;
All, all are gone, the old familiar faces."

To return to memories of my mother; the experiences of two world wars, and the long illness of my father, brought confirmation of the real courage and staunchness of purpose that underlay her gentle appearance and diffident manner. An incident in the second world war illustrates this, as did her dutiful endurance in the first.

My work took me away from home during the first year, of the so-called 'phoney' war, but I returned just as the bombing started. My father was in relatively good health at that time, and became an Air Raid Warden. He had to act as look-out on the roofs of buildings, inspect the underground shelters, and patrol the blacked-out streets. Gigantic searchlights swept the skies, crossing and recrossing each other, probing the clouds and outshining the stars, in search of enemy bombers. These latter favoured moonlight nights, but for a period in 1941 they came over in waves promptly at six each evening.

We were under their flight-path on their way to the Manchester Docks and industrial area, and as the ack-ack guns defending the docks drove many of them back, the suburbs had the benefit of their jettisoned bombs.

Fortunately, because of the nature of my work (Organising the Emergency Feeding for bombed-out people and the Housewives' Education Campaign) and of my father's part-time duties, the Authorities had had our cellar reinforced for us. We happened to have a lavatory and a coal-fire down there, and when the sirens sounded, we descended with a picnic supper to our camp-beds below; and this went on for six months.

One night when my father was out on duty a land-mine fell near us, and the blast surprisingly blew in the heavy cellar door, which fell across the foot of my mother's bed. The crash was appalling, and the cellar was filled with the roar of the bombers and the red glow of burning buildings. We managed to move the door, and my mother, murmuring "How noisy it is", lay down and instantly settled to sleep again. I was anxious about my father's safety, but too nervous to go upstairs or outside until the raiders had gone.

My father returned at daybreak, and we found the top of the house intact, even the roof and chimneys; but every window was shattered, and the curtains, including the inner black-out ones, were torn to shreds. Heaps of broken glass, soot and plaster lay everywhere. My mother rose early, and after shedding a few tears at "the worry of it all", she set to work to sweep up the glass and rubbish, and to find blankets and rugs to hang at the windows.

Though not as bad as the Christmas fire blitz, it was one of the city's worst. Transport was disrupted, and everywhere people were walking to work through toppled masonry and piles of rubble and snaking hosepipes.

BOMB STORY . . MANCHESTER, 1942

For a year we lived like troglodytes,
Then a landmine, a near miss,
Blew in the cellar-door.
It flattened my mother's camp-bed.
She rolled under the next one,
Murmured, "How noisy",
And slept peacefully on.

The rectangle of the skeleton doorway
Framed a crimson furnace. . . the city on fire,
Under the lowering weight of an endless heavy roar
Of the bombers circling. . .'theirs', of course;
And over that the booming racket of the ack-ack guns. .
'Ours', thank heaven!

Our neighbour descended two floors in her bed
Unhurt; two others were buried.
Another, away for the night,
Rushed home and found it a smoking ruin.
Her mother's Chippendale sideboard,
A few charred fragments. . was what
Caused her abandonment to helpless tears.

Our windows were all shattered, every one;
The curtains shredded into long vertical strips,
Like the tattered colours of a regiment
After honourable battle.
Our neighbour's garden had a crater that would hold
                                        two buses.
He said the rich soil thrown up was most productive,
And round the perimeter he grew excellent lettuces
The next spring of the war.
Meanwhile, his wife's lace corselet and her mended red
                                        jumper
Hung forty feet up in an elm
Whose leaves were scorched off.

Next morning a Pompeiian pall of dust and smoke
Loomed over all, with hosepipes snaking
Slimily in black mud across the thoroughfares.
One errant spray,
Trespassing into our too, too-open windows
Unkindly moistened our National bread and marge,
Our ersatz coffee, and soya porridge,
And straw-pale tea.

But everywhere you could hear the cheerful tinkling
Of broken glass as housewives swept it up
Into neat heaps on their garden paths;
One bemoaning her Persian carpet's ruin;
Another the grit on her drawing-room settee.

But at seven sharp the milk was on the step,
And at seven-thirty the newsboy came cycling,
Zigzagging among the firemen;
Whistling, surprisingly, an air from a Nocturne of
                                        Chopin. . .
The most beautiful sound in the world.

I found my office window, too, in fragments on the
floor, and as the building next door was still on fire, spray
from the firemen's hoses kept watering the papers on my
desk.

But I had a pleasant surprise: a colleague brought a present in for me. It was a cardboard shoe-box lined with cotton-wool, and nestling inside were two cooking apples, a Spanish onion, and two fresh eggs. I don't know how he came by them, but they were among the almost endless list of unobtainable foods, and my mother was delighted.

And that reminds me of another unusual gift. The main door of the offices had some splendid stained glass panels, and these too were blown to bits. The Chief Accountant happened to find in the rubble several hundred yards from the office, the circular central medallion or plaque, surrounded by its lead border, perfectly intact. He preserved it, and when he retired at Christmas he gave it to me; a lovely Burne-Jones design, it hangs still in my hall window, a souvenir of stressful but exciting times.

Stressful they certainly were for my mother; but in spite of the wreckage all round, and the death of three neighbours in the demolished houses, she pulled herself together, never showed her anxieties, and carried on doggedly, as in the 1914 war, through further years of perils and privations. Was this the mother who had imparted so many nervous fears to us in our childhood?

When I think of her now, in my own old age, I reflect on her real inner self, not the tense, over-anxious mother-self. I see her tending her plants, working at her embroidery, caring for our clothing, or seated at her piano, or graciously receiving guests at her "At Homes".

What a sad pity it is that we cannot always react to our mothers, in childhood and in adolescence, with the understanding, sympathy, and with a modicum of the wisdom and balance which, we hope, comes to us with the years!